I0754897

# PILLAR

# TO POST

SAM WRIGHT

GOST

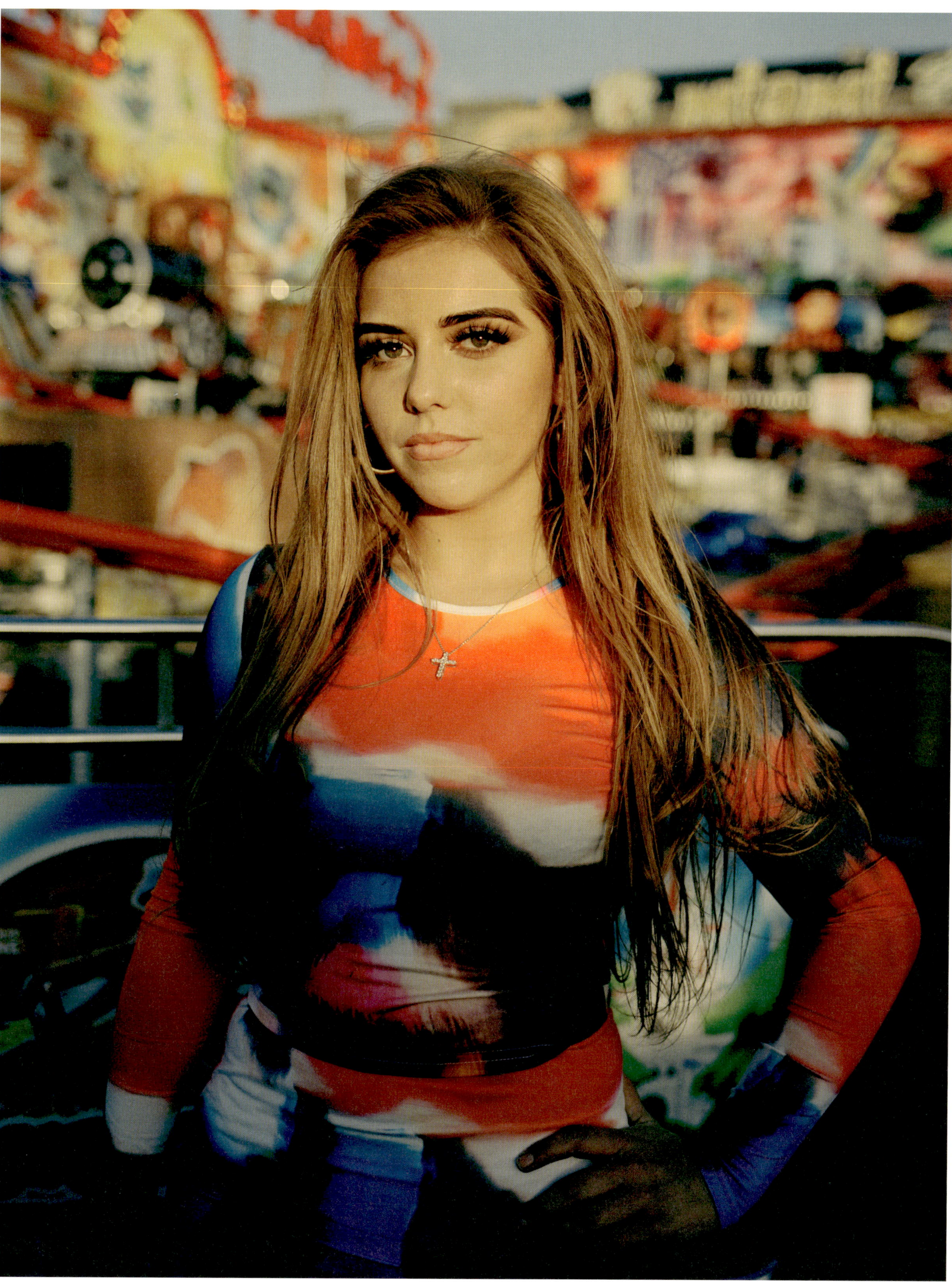

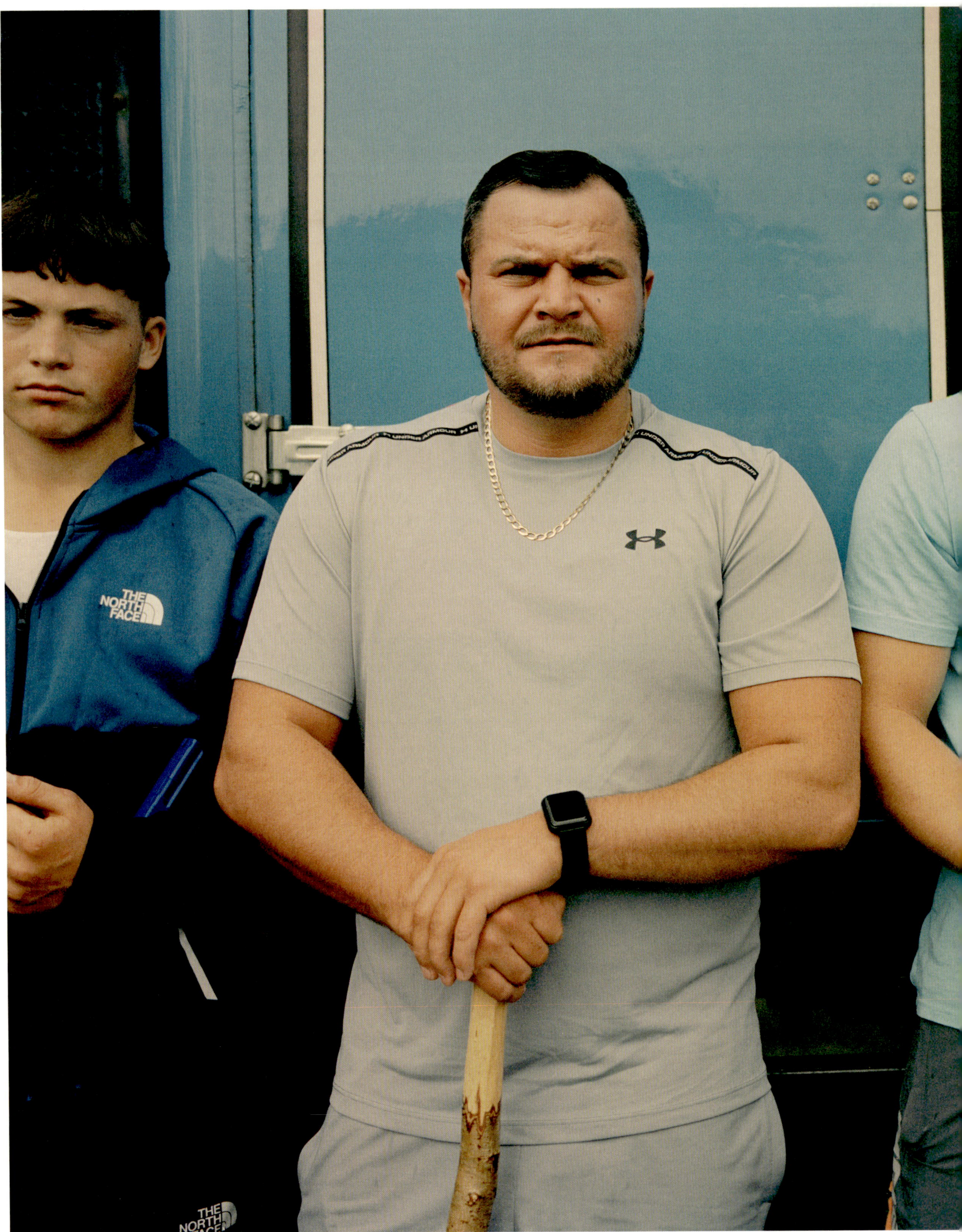
THE NORTH FACE
UNDER ARMOUR

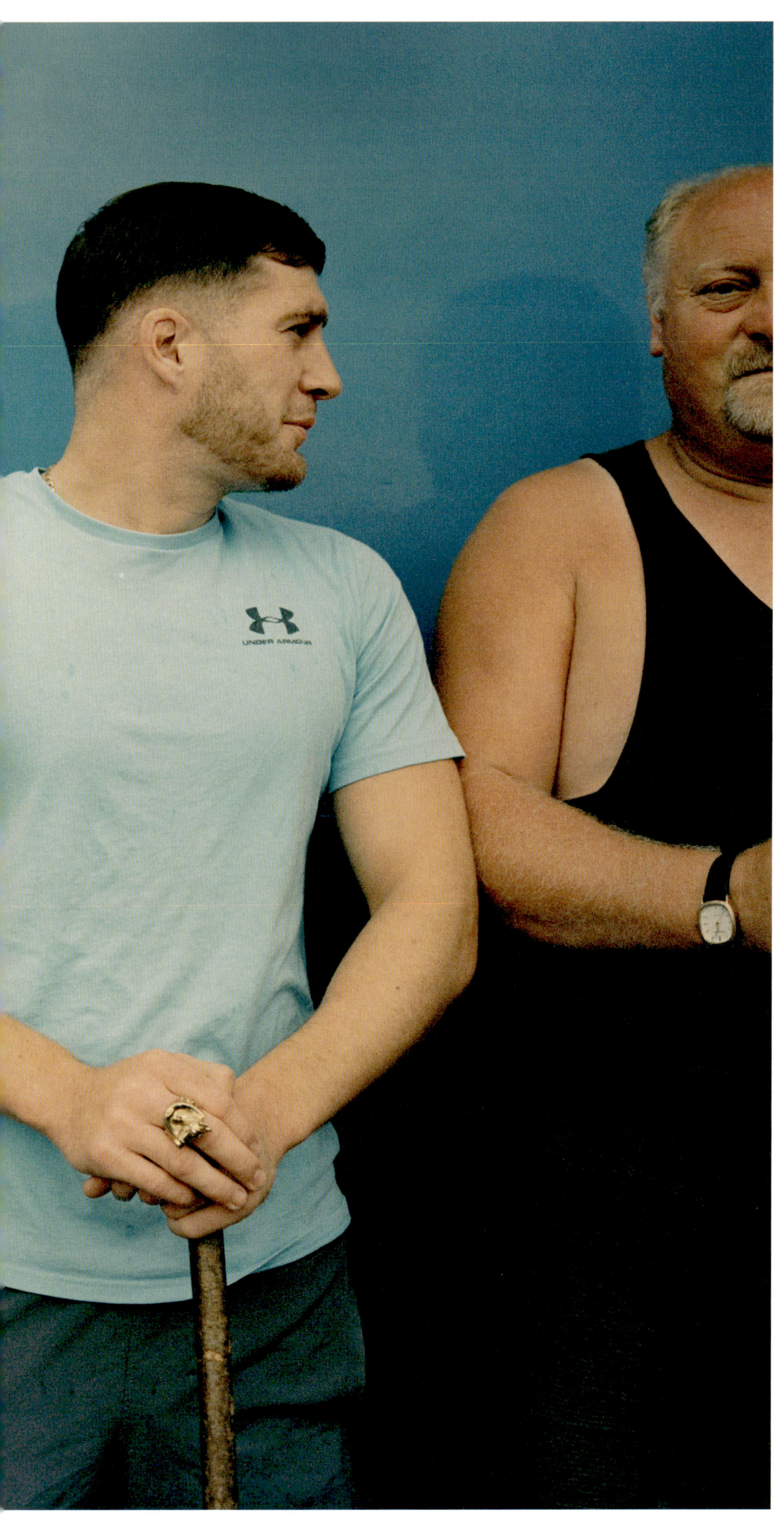
UNDER ARMOUR

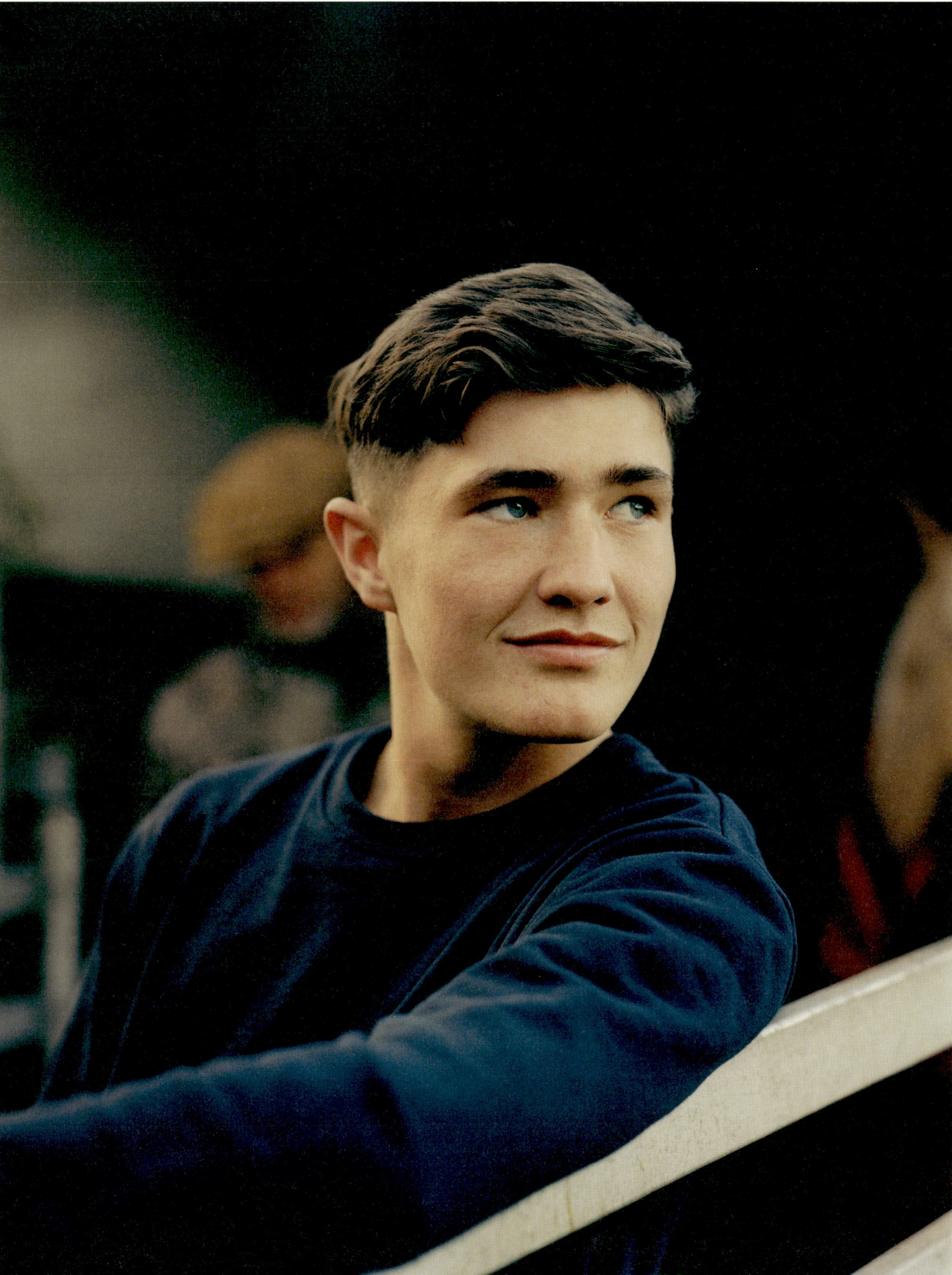

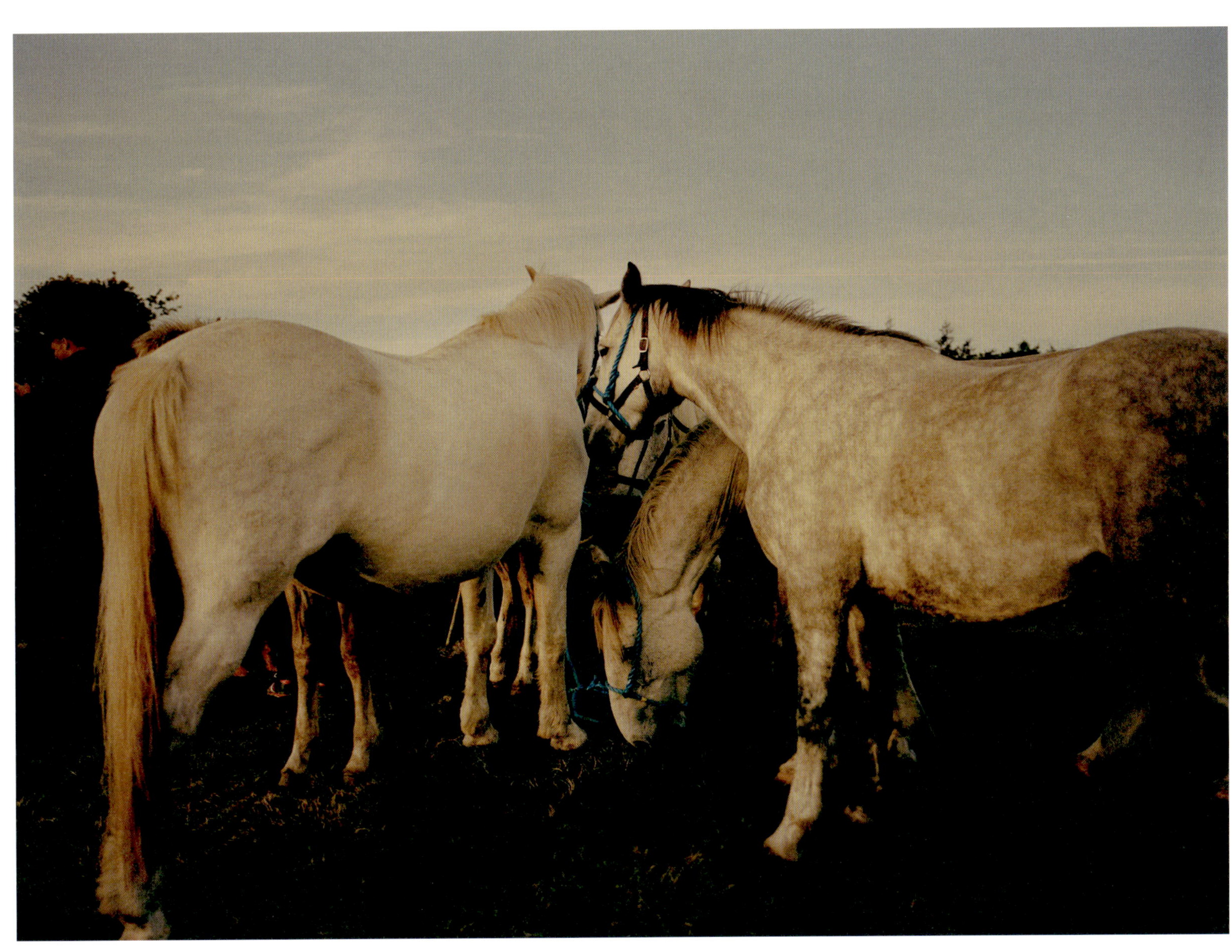

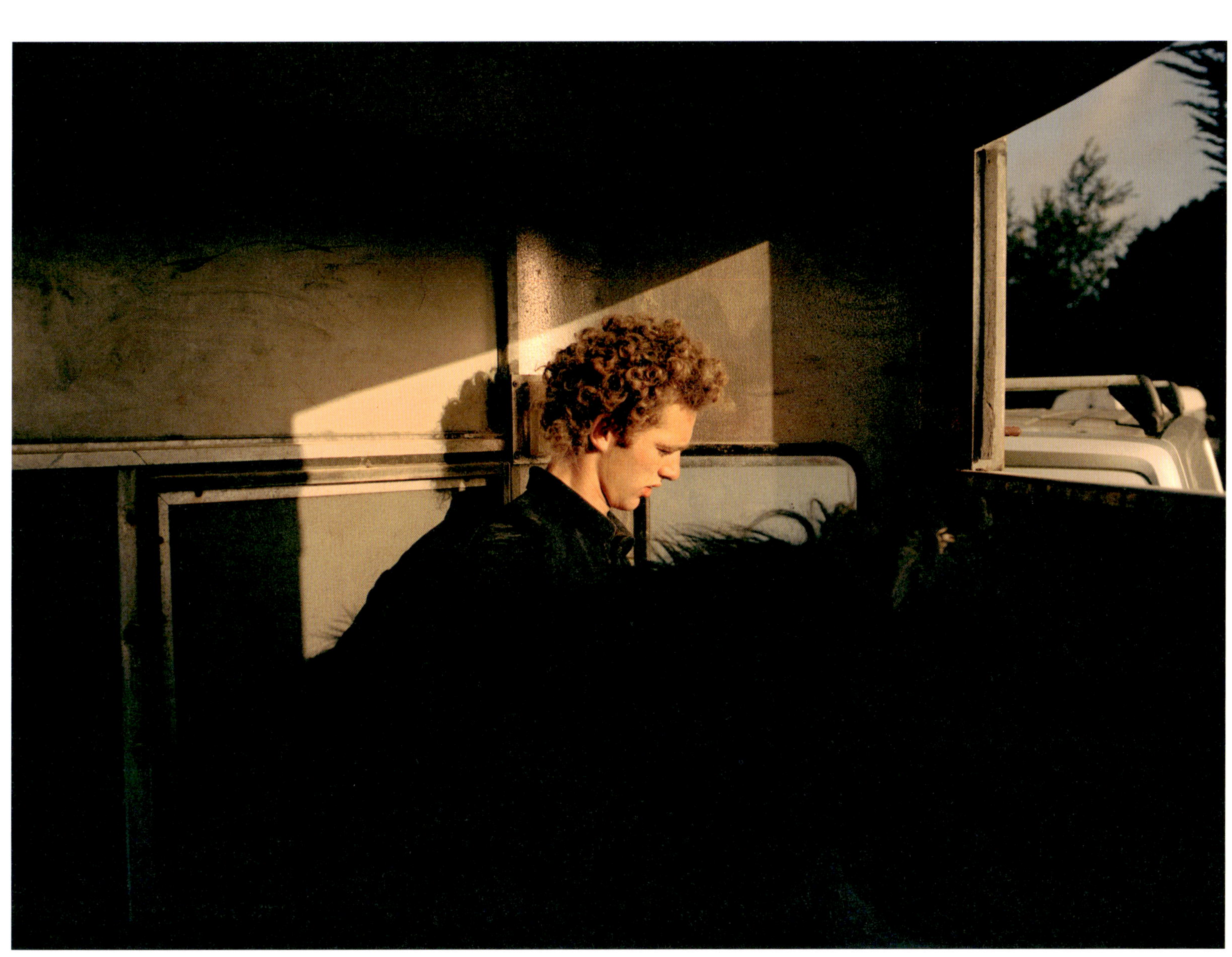

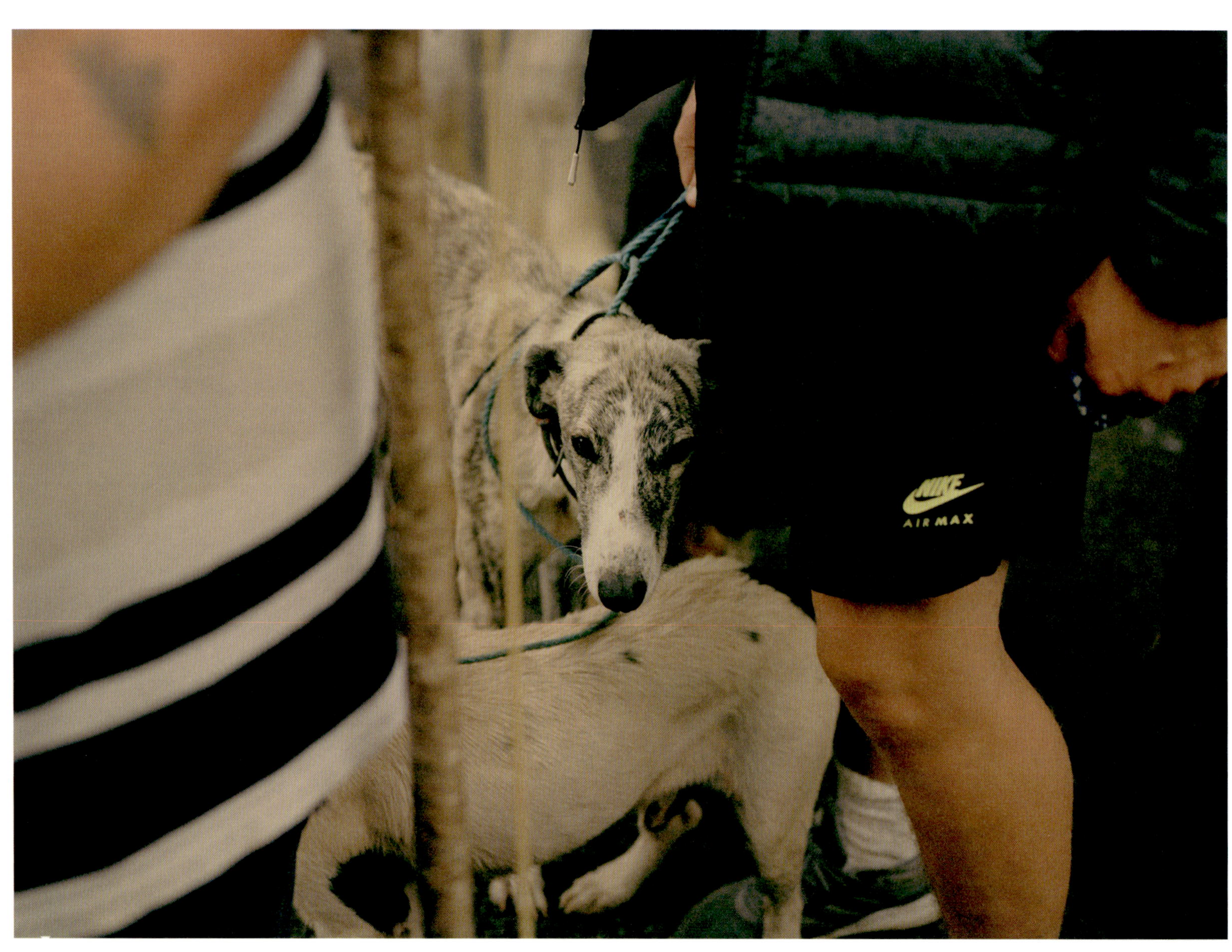
NIKE
AIR MAX

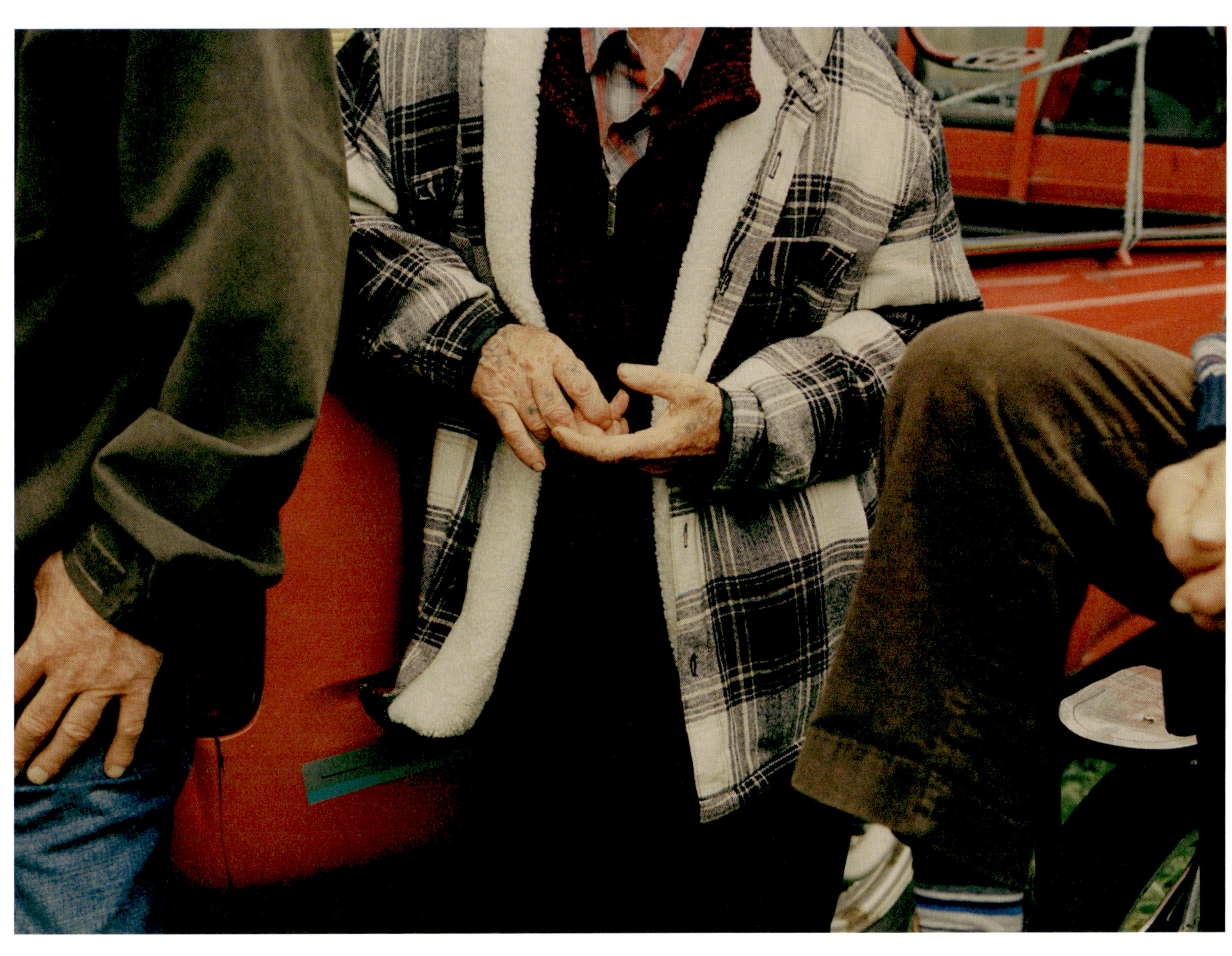

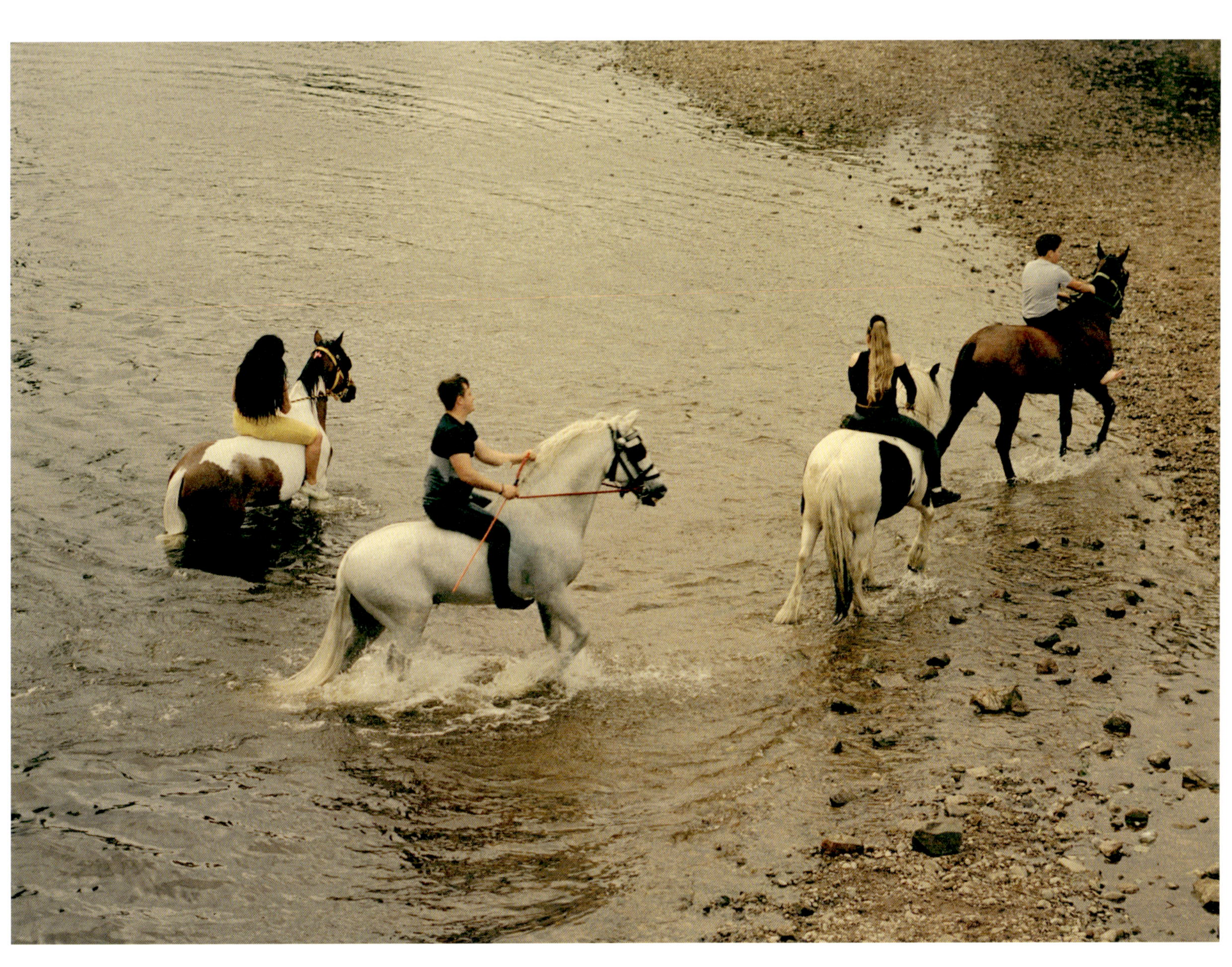

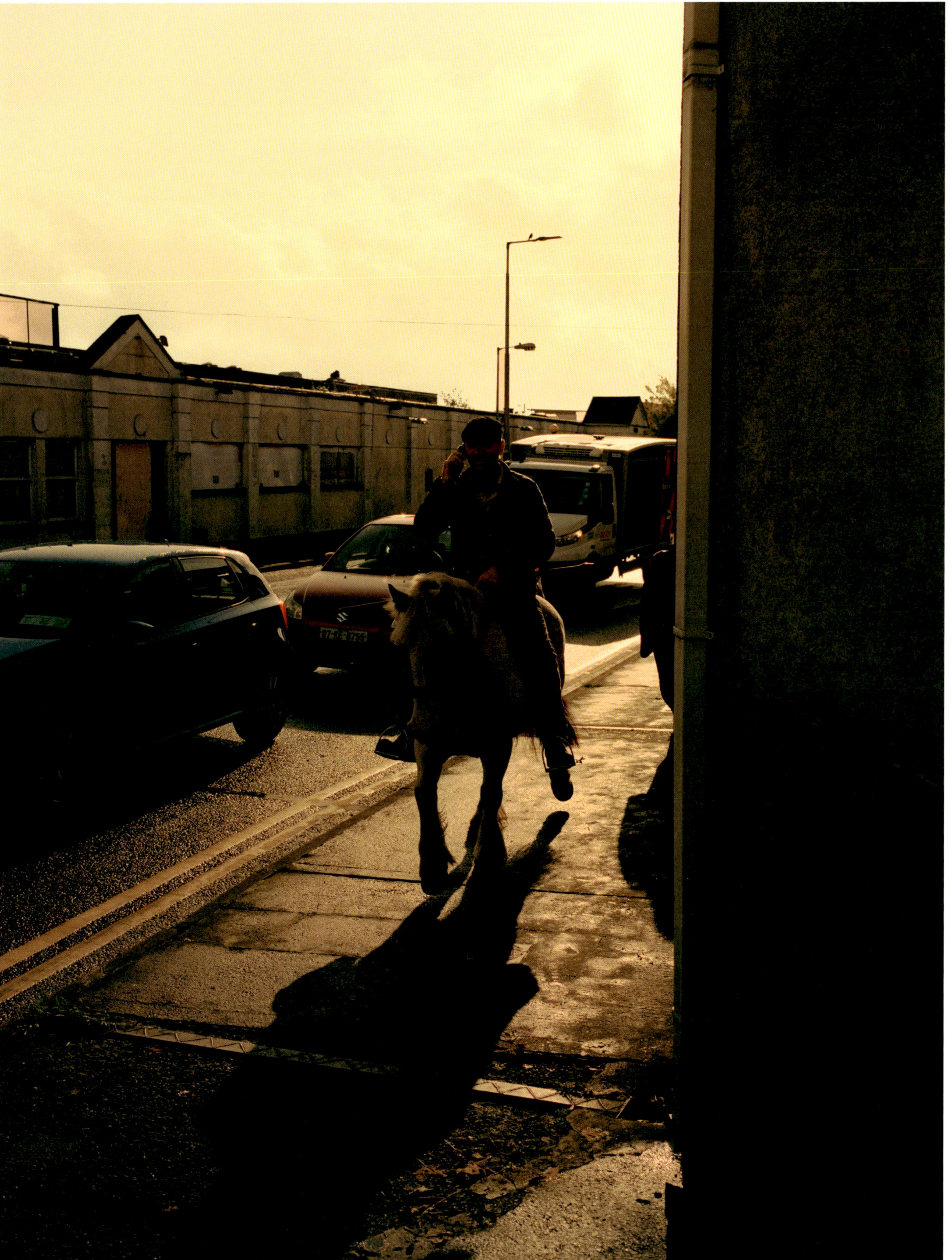

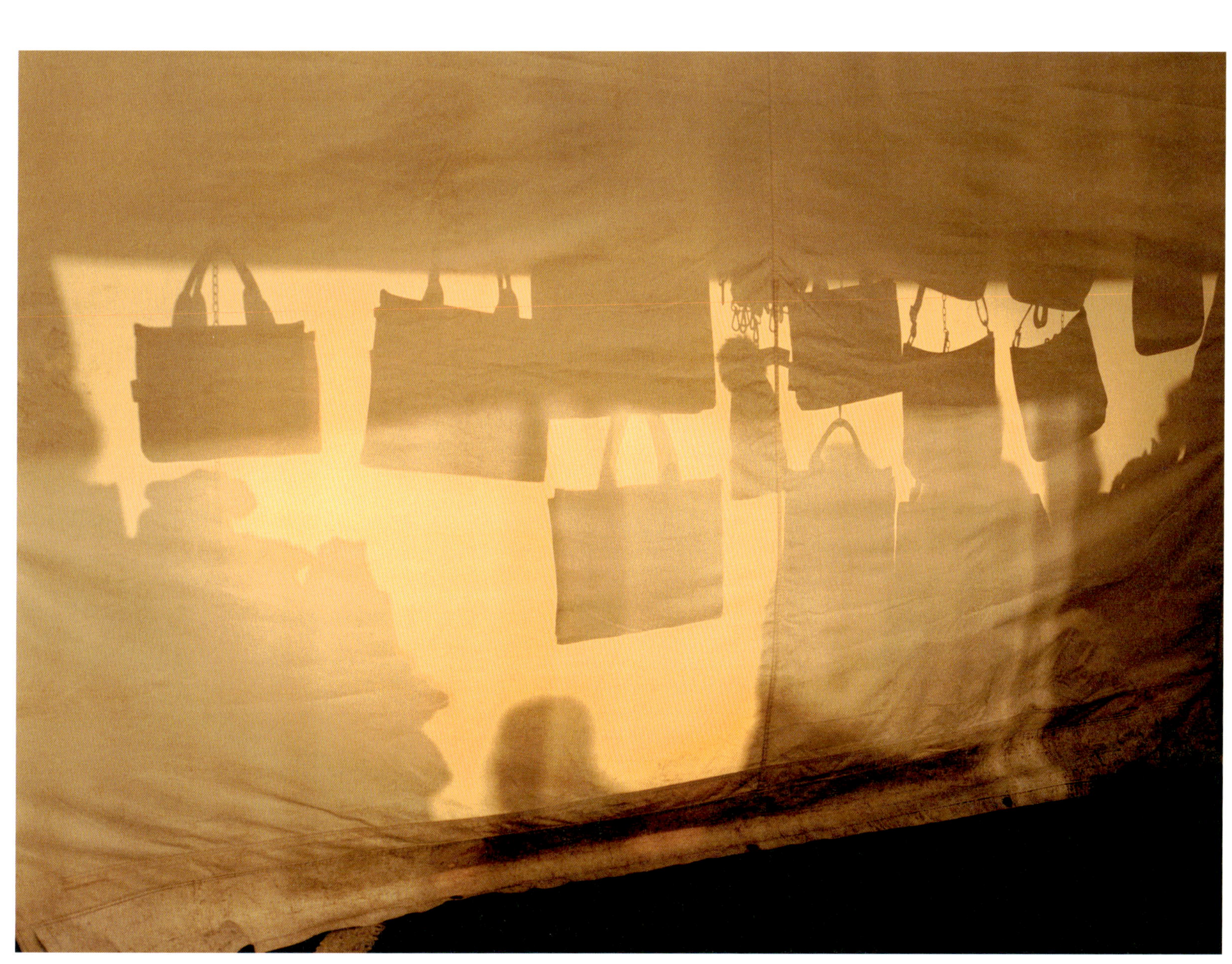

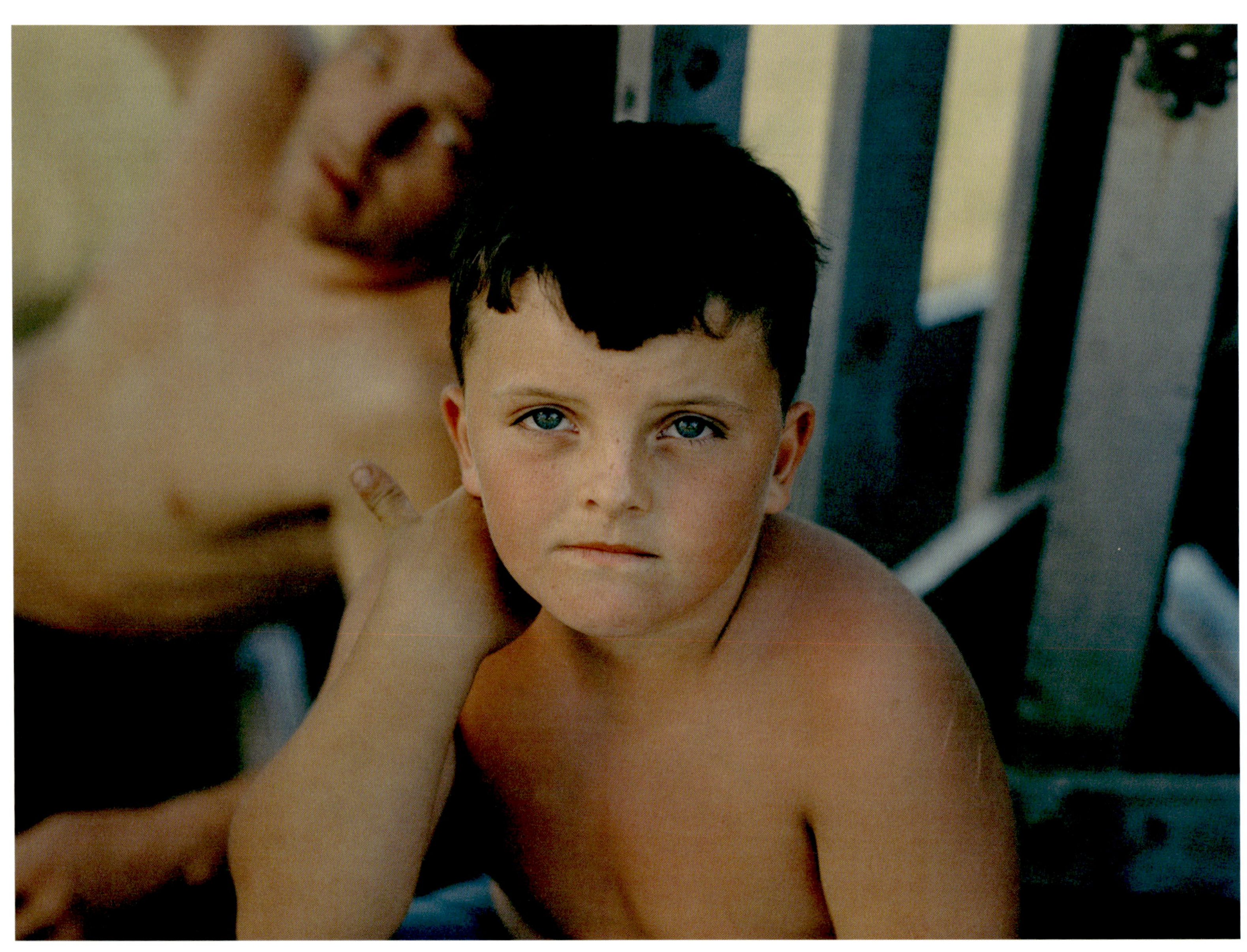

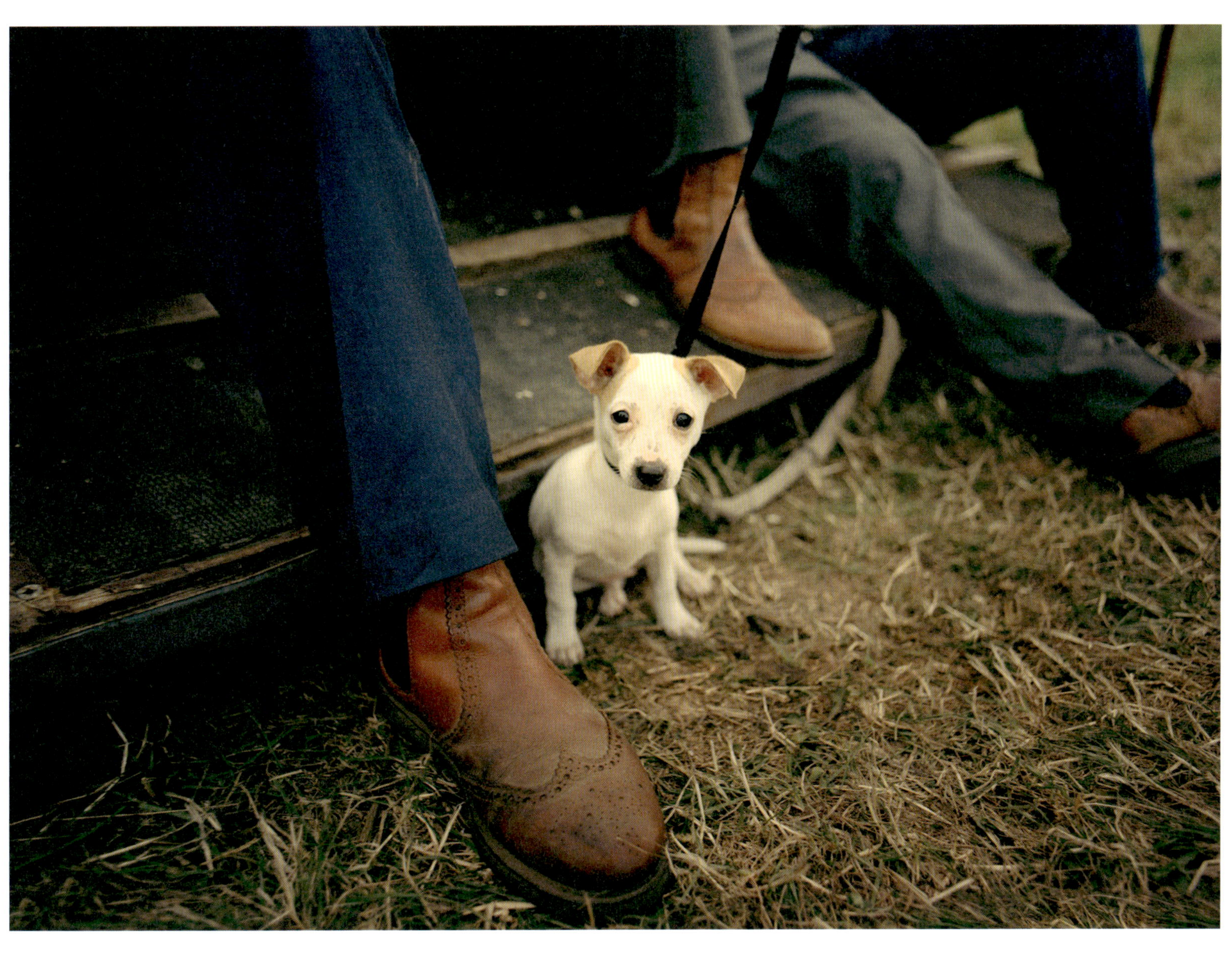

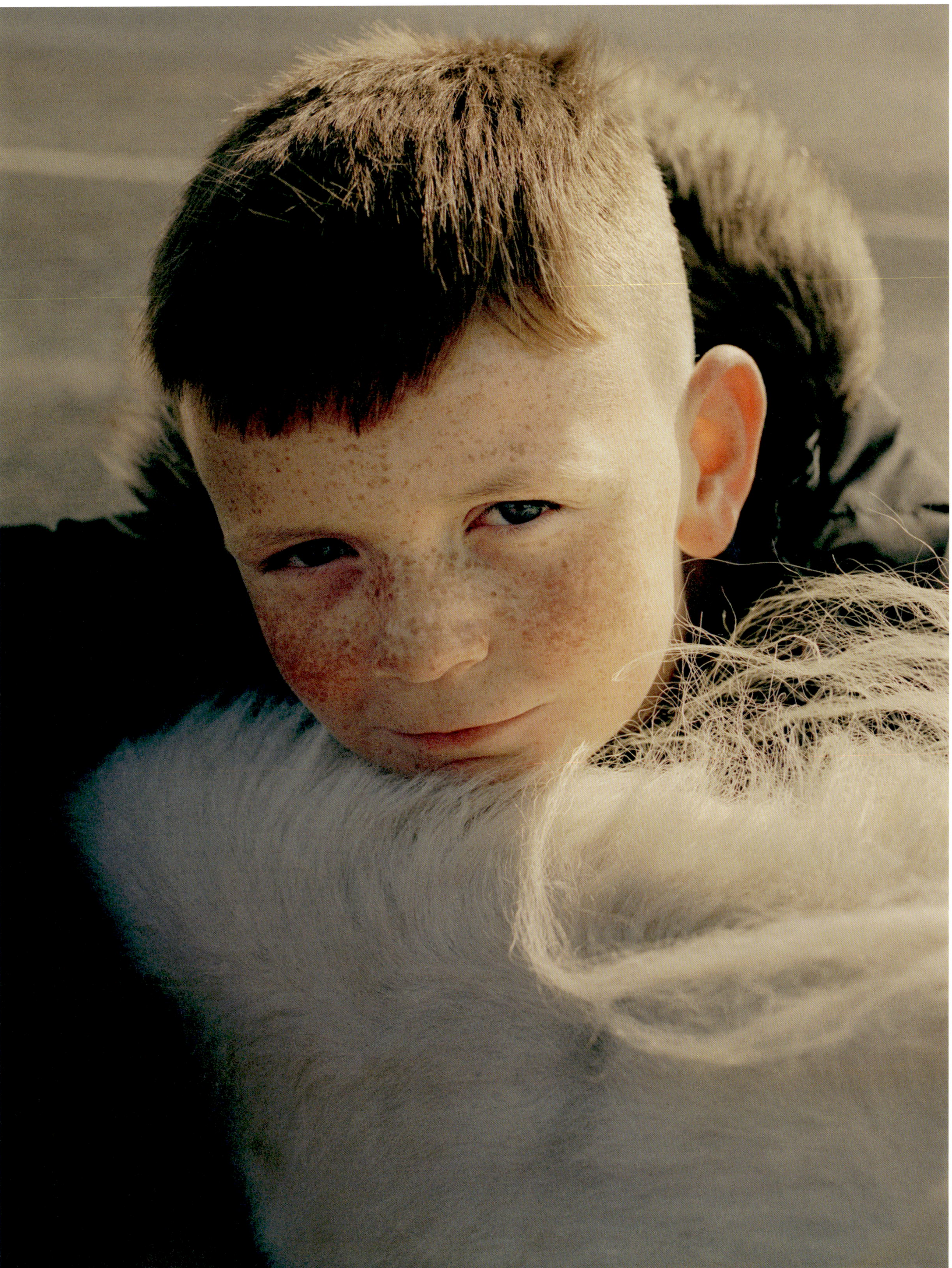

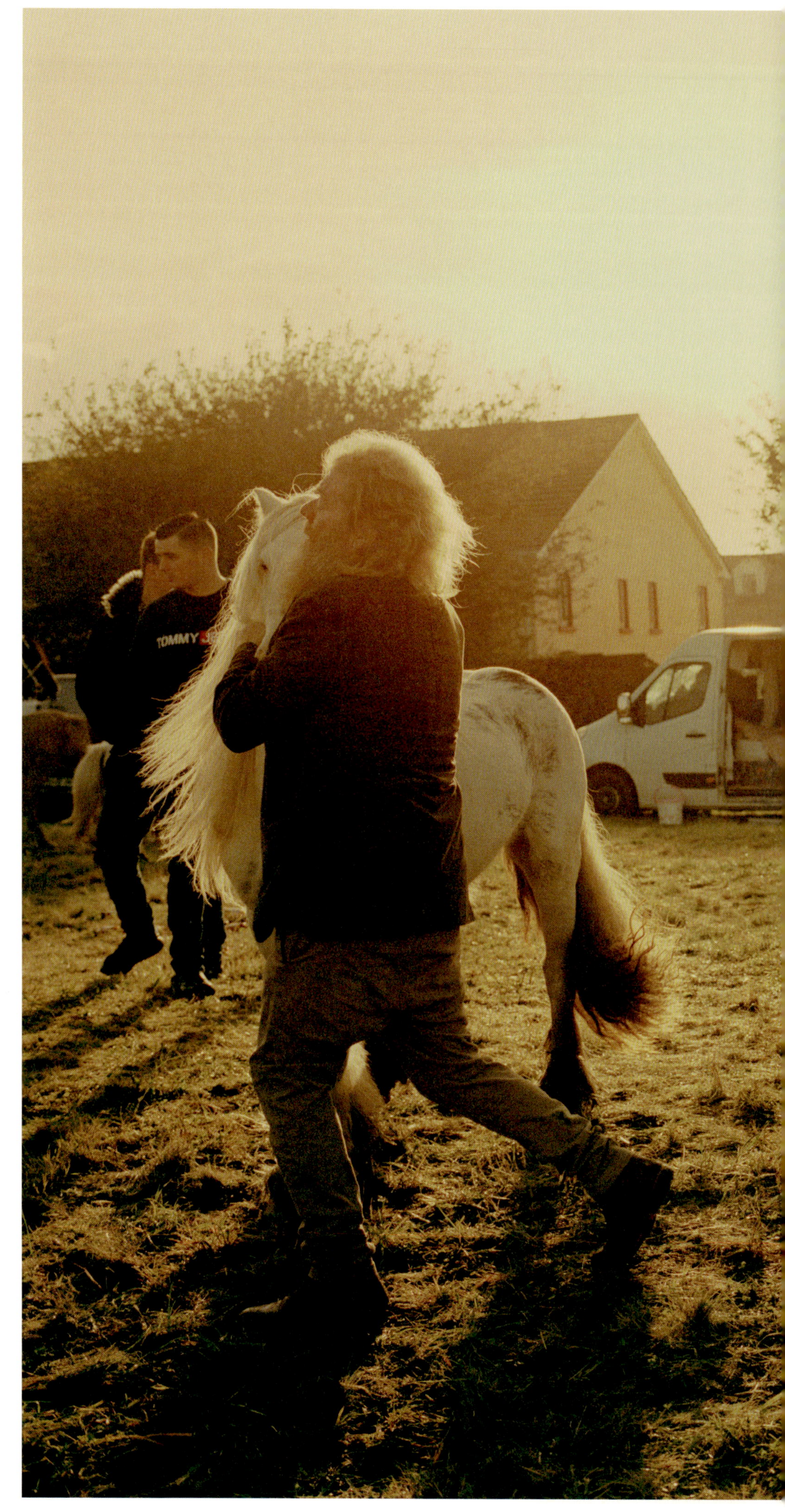
TOMMY

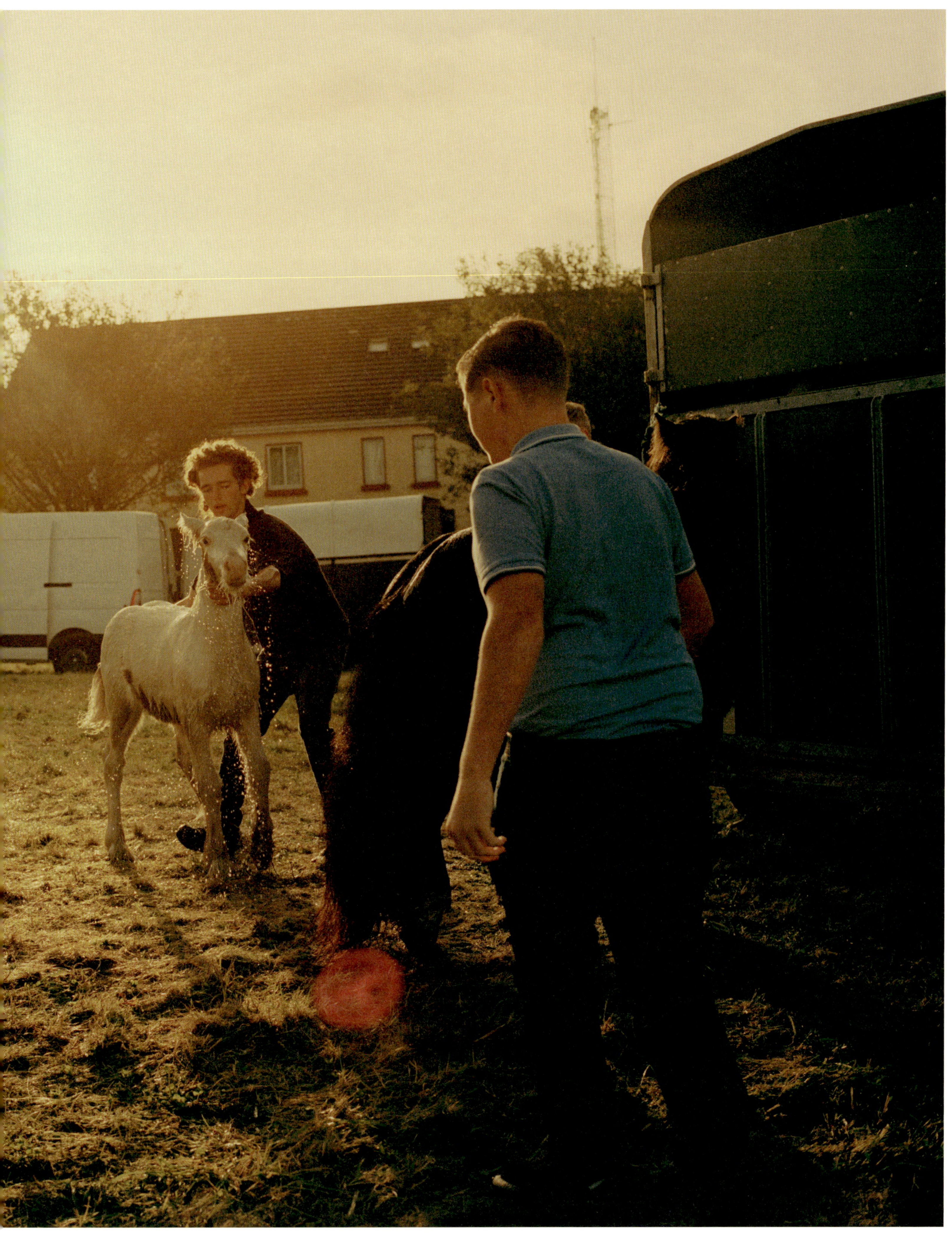

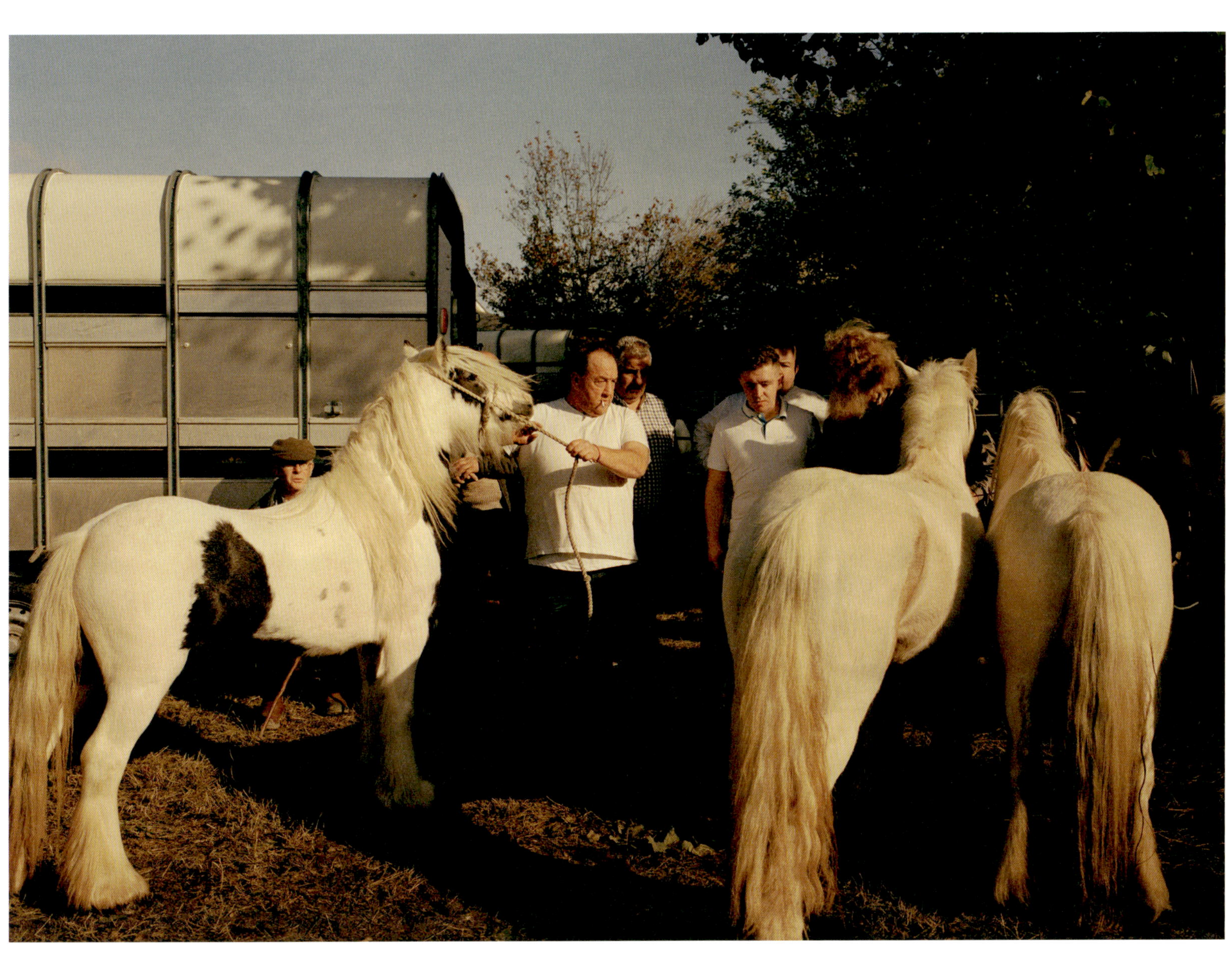

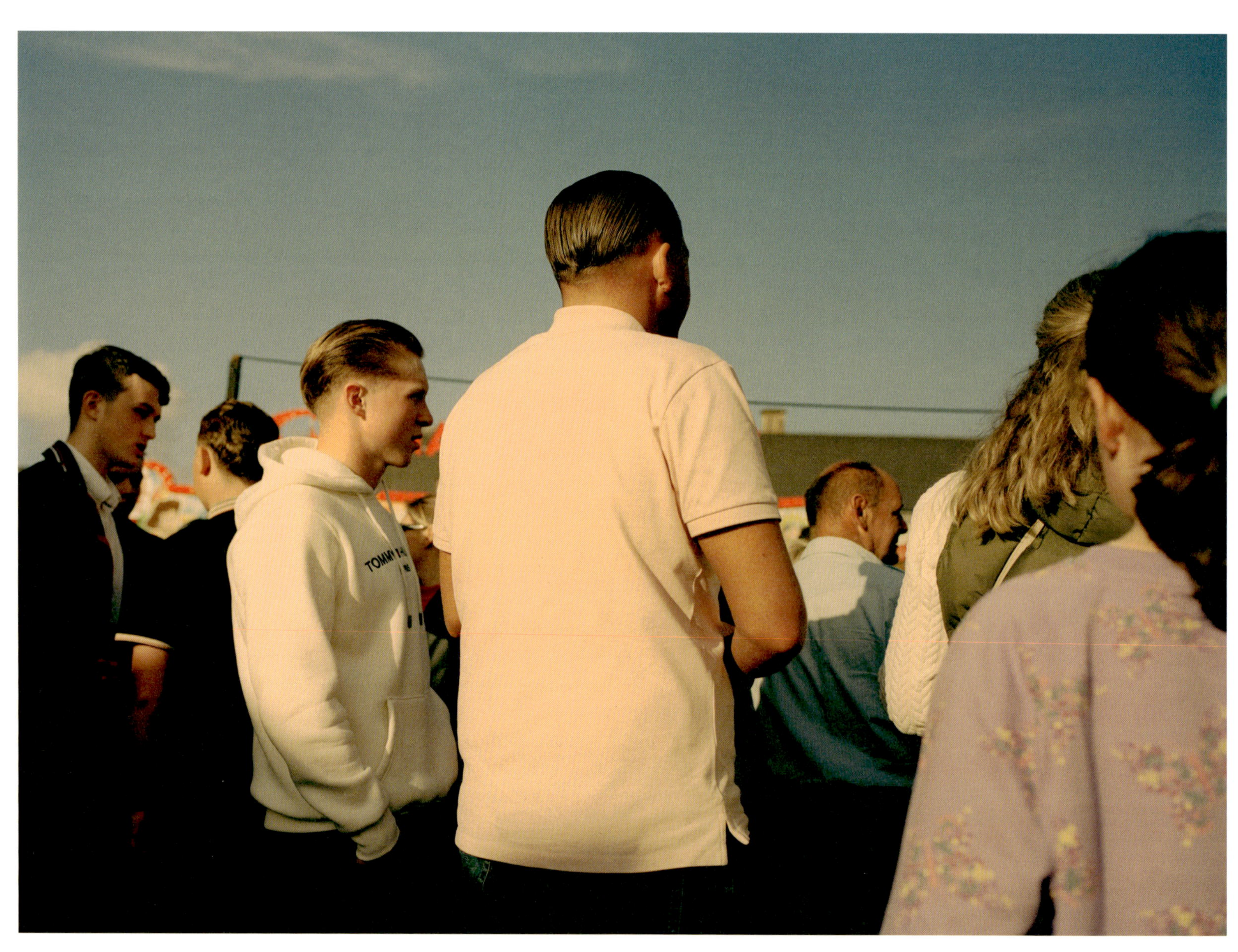
TOMMY

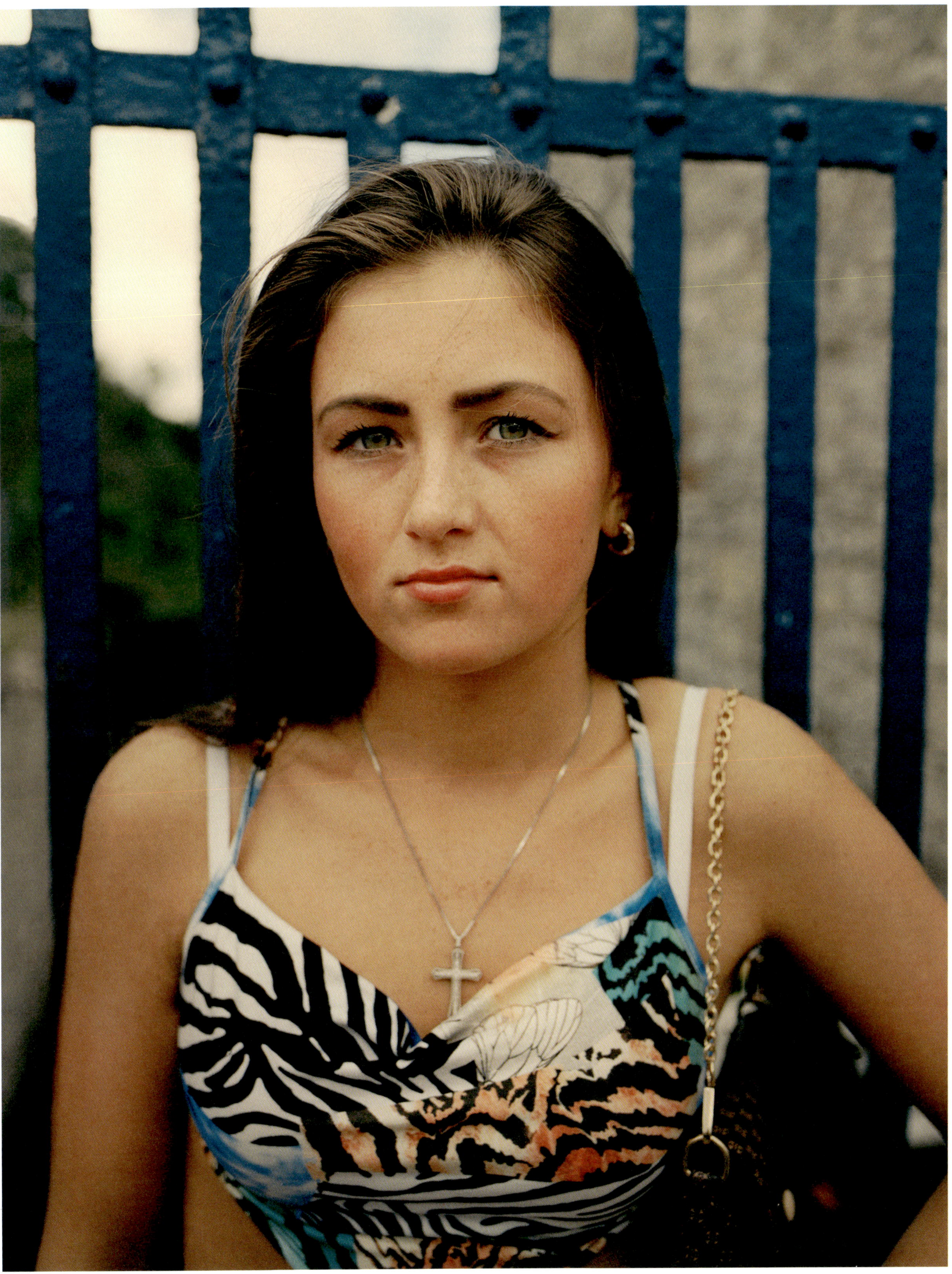

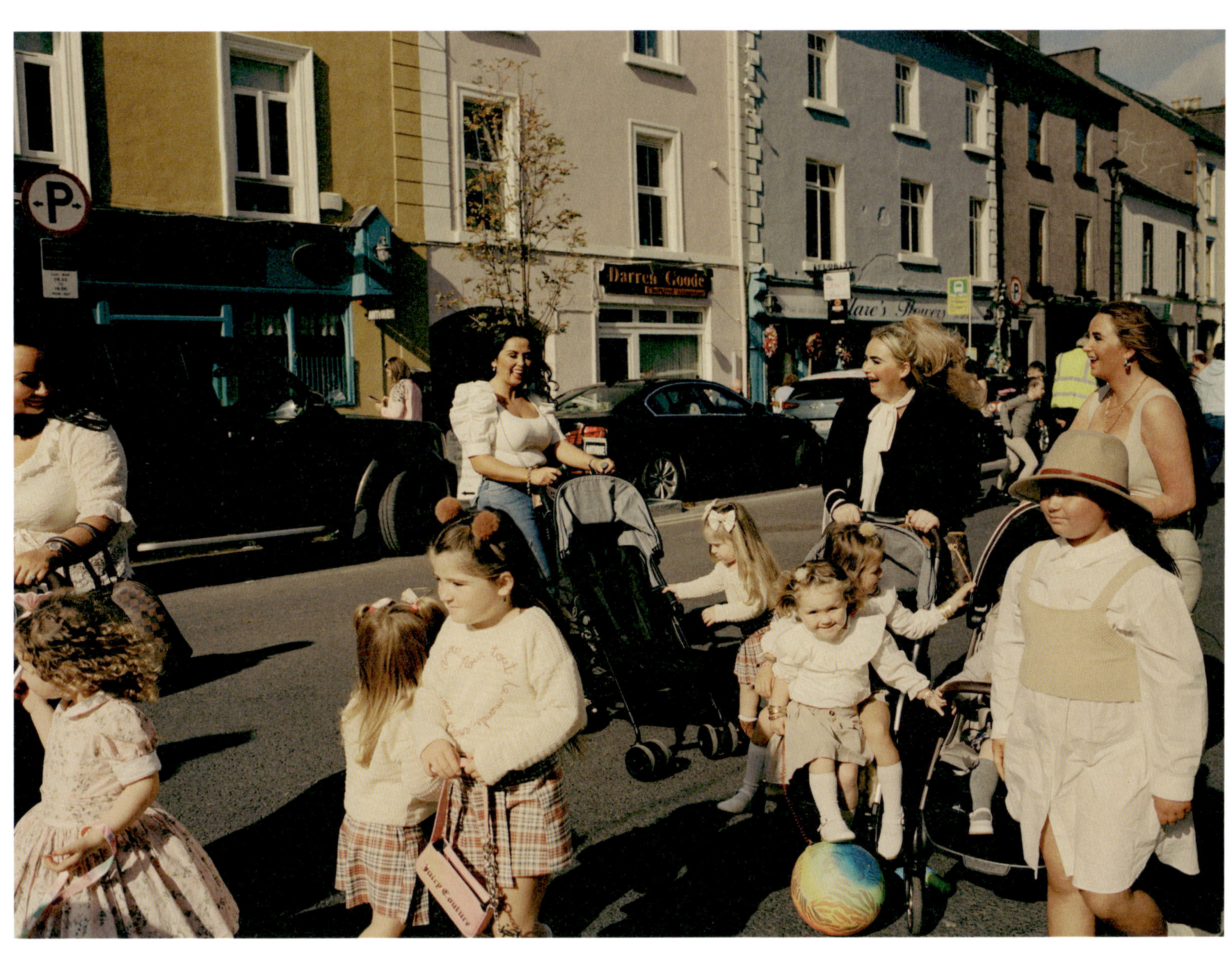
Darren Goode

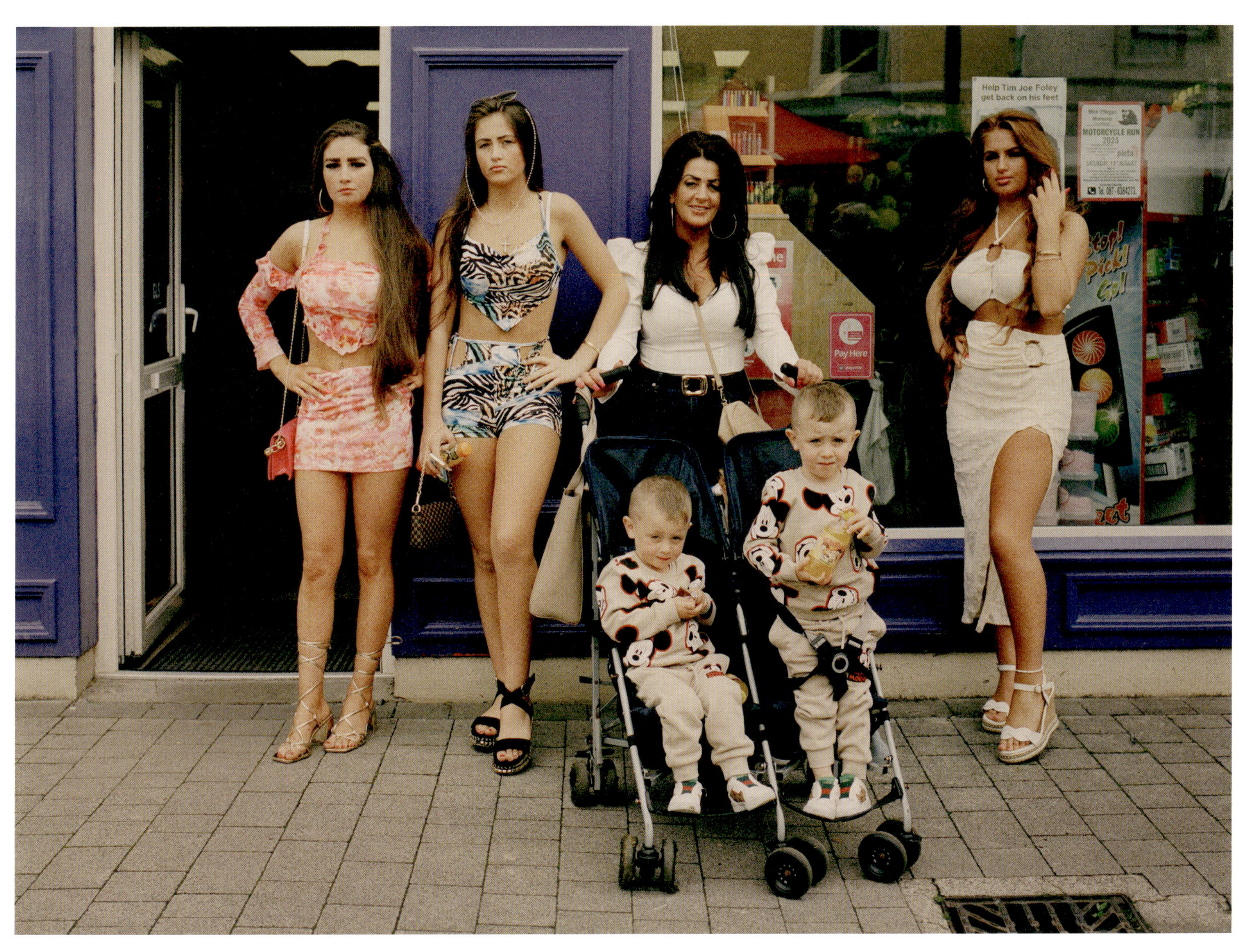
Help Tim Joe Foley
get back on his feet
MOTORCYCLE RUN
2023
pieta
Pay Here
Stop!
Pick!
Go!

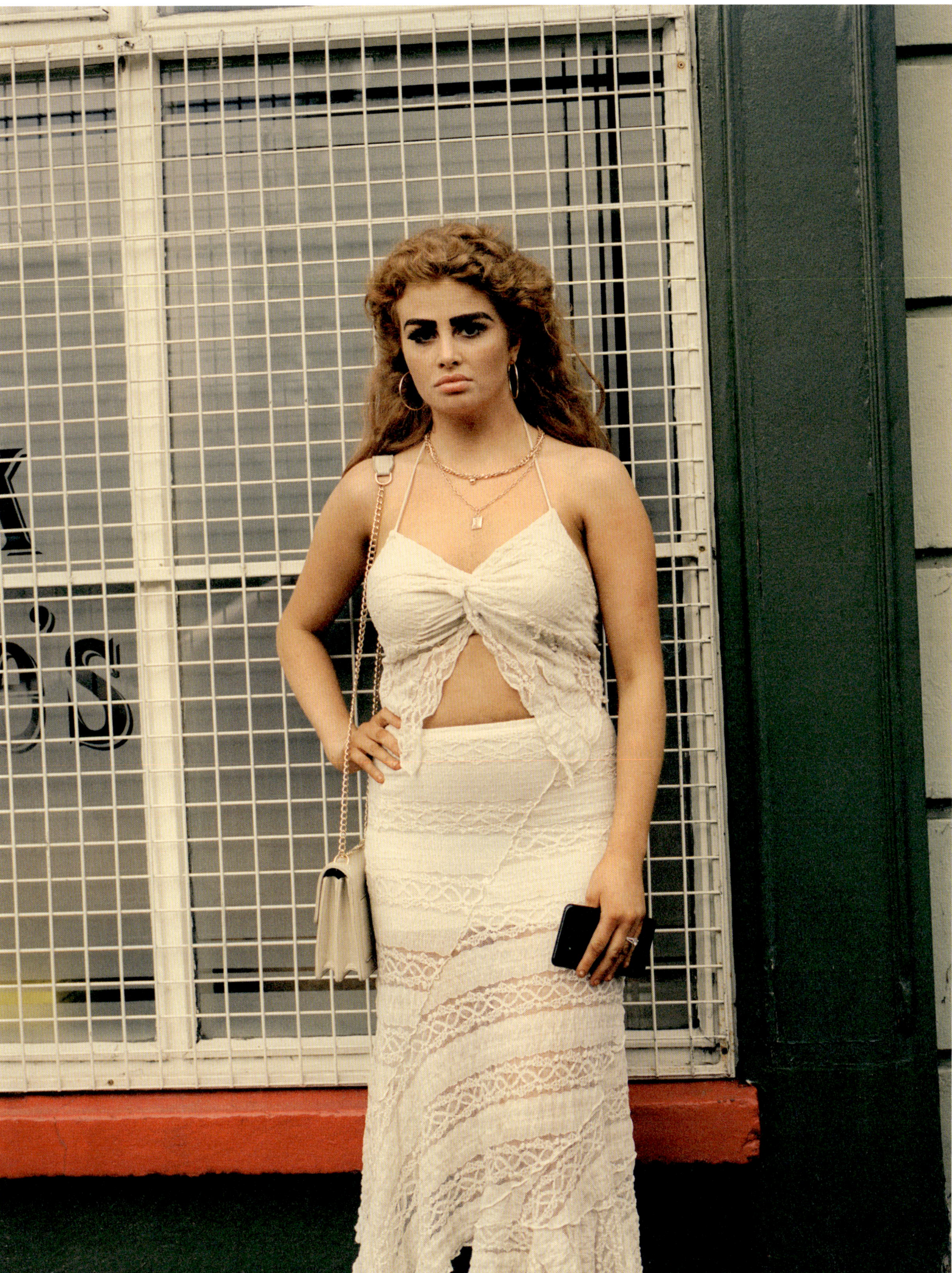

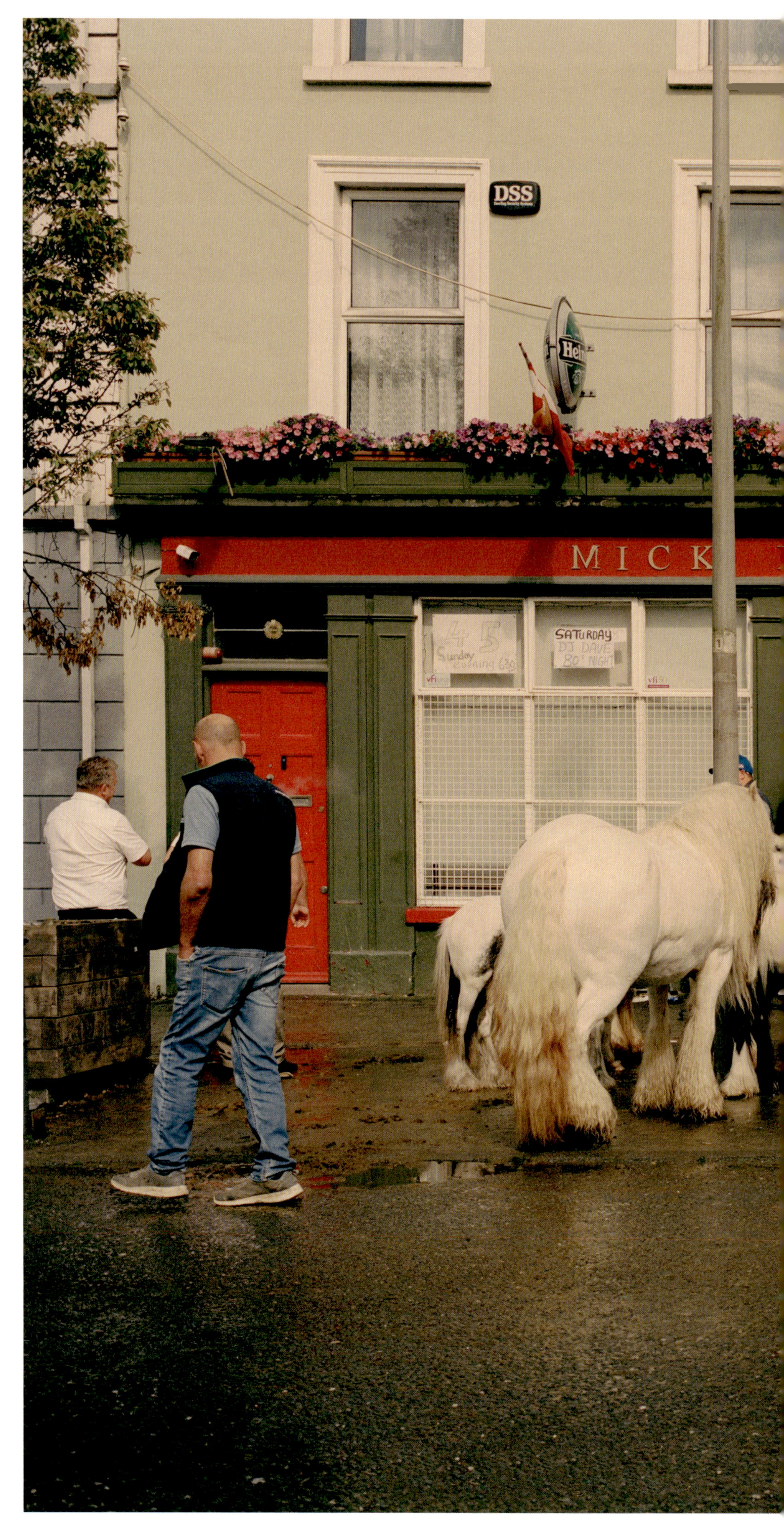
DSS
MICK
45
Sunday
evening 6.30
SATURDAY
DJ DAVE
80' NIGHT

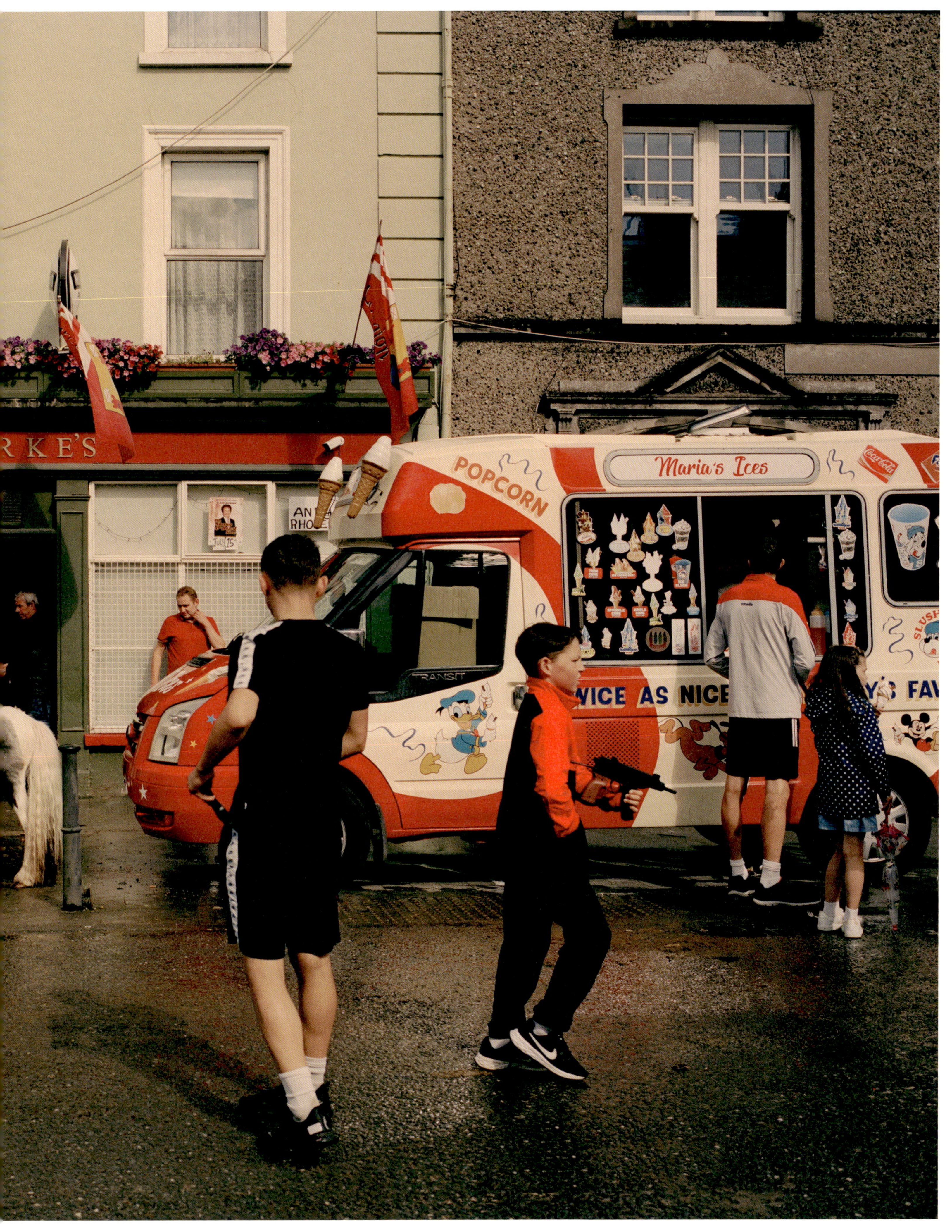
RKE'S
POPCORN
Maria's Ices
Coca-Cola
TRANSIT
WICE AS NICE
SLUSH

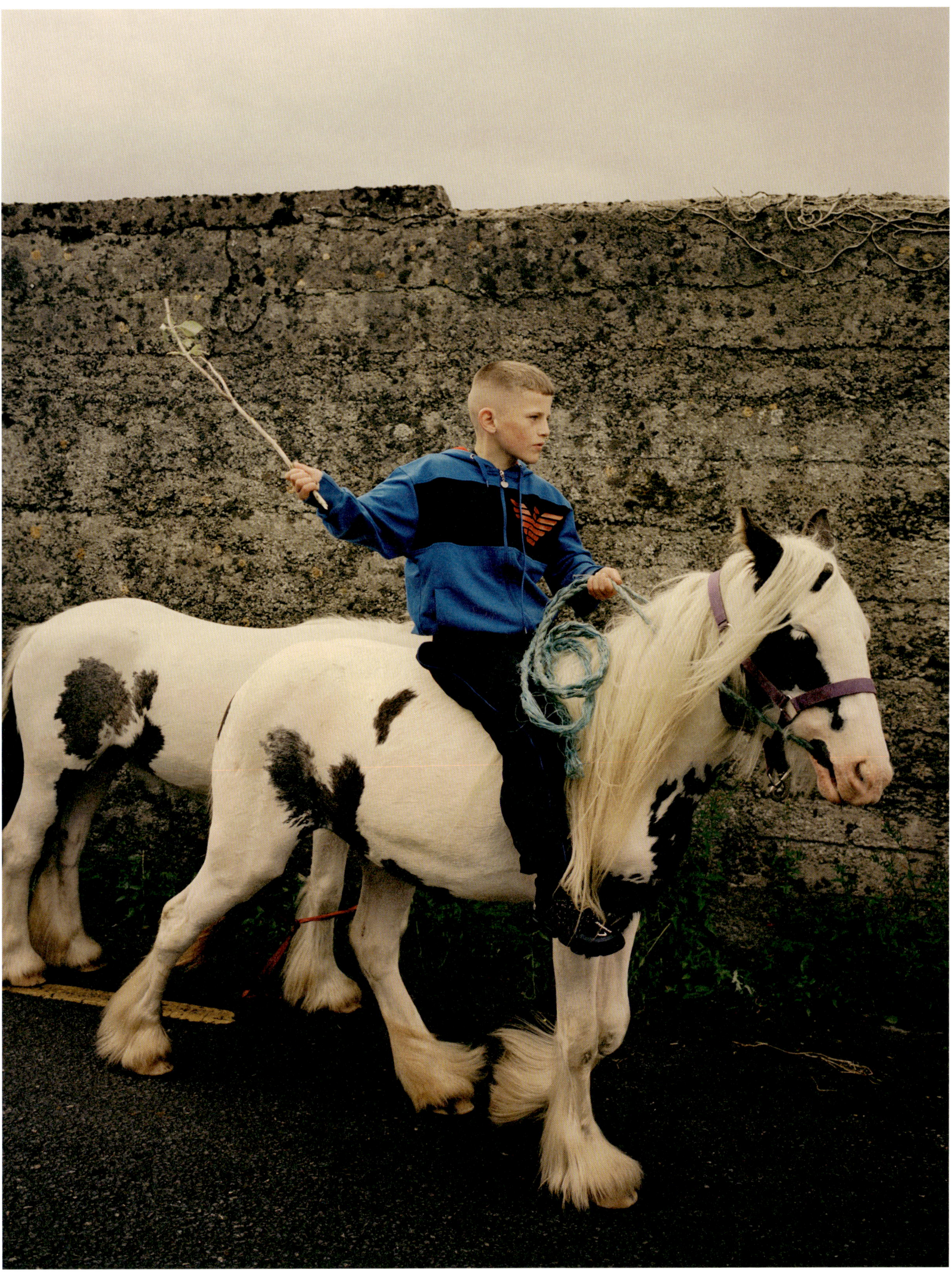

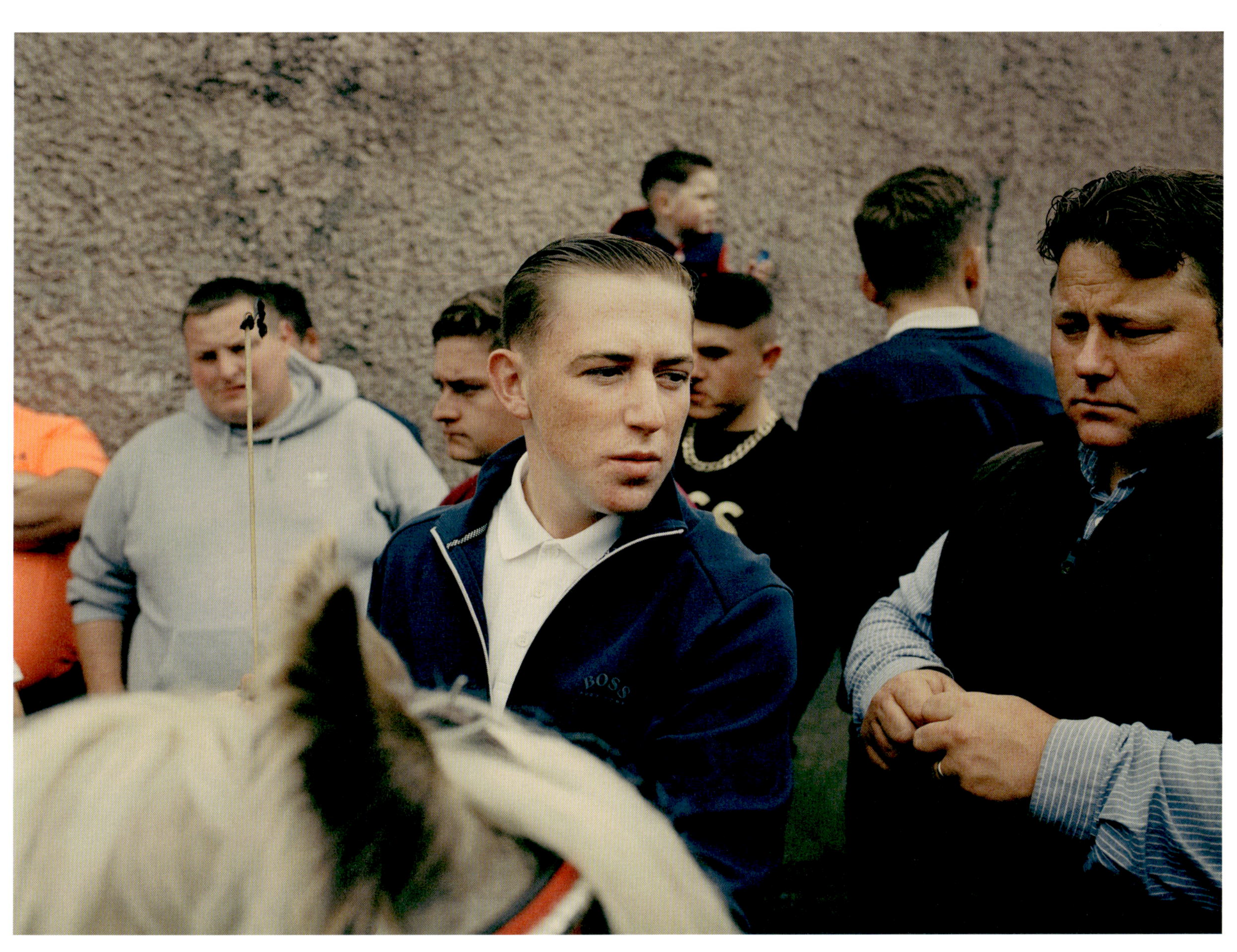
BOSS

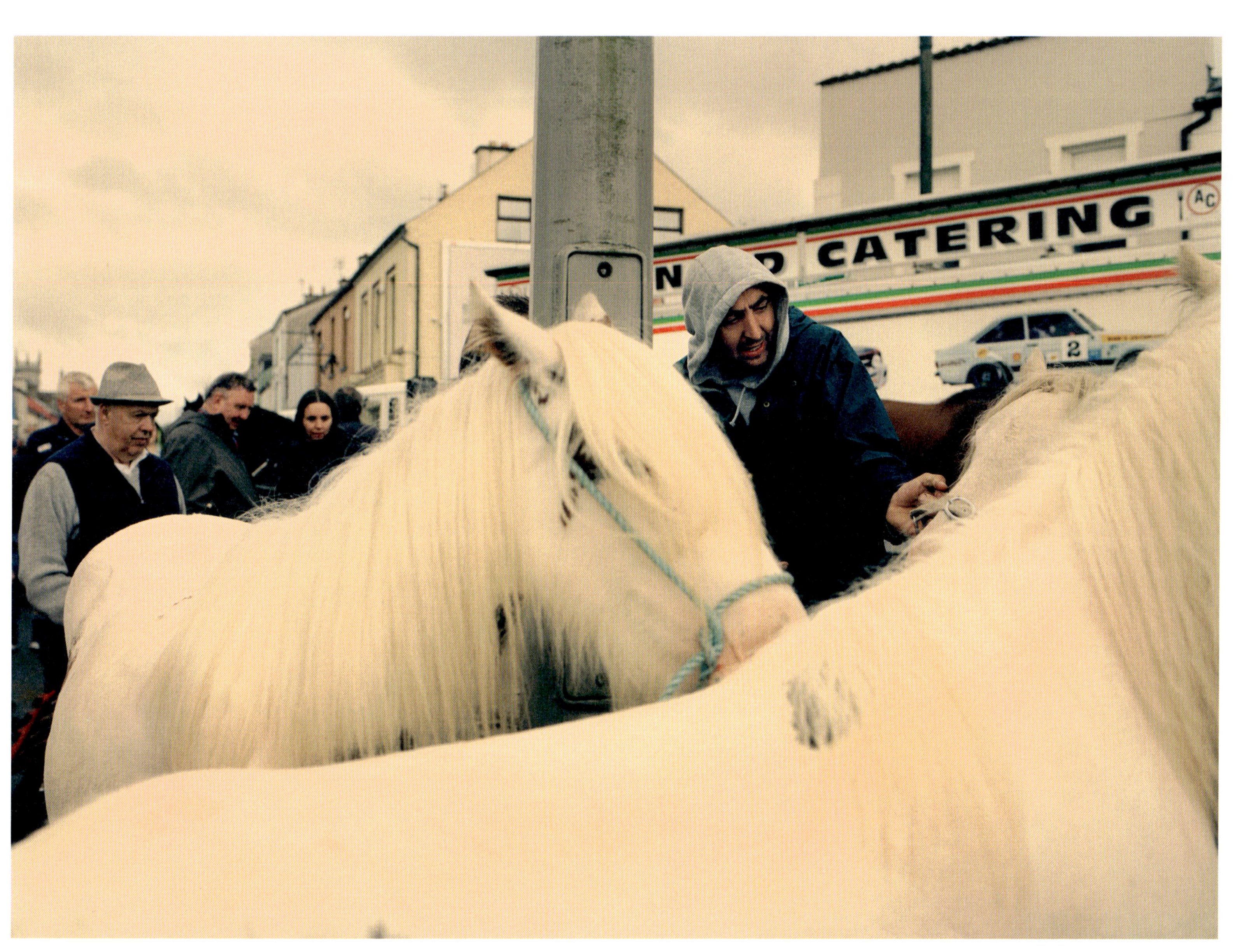
CATERING

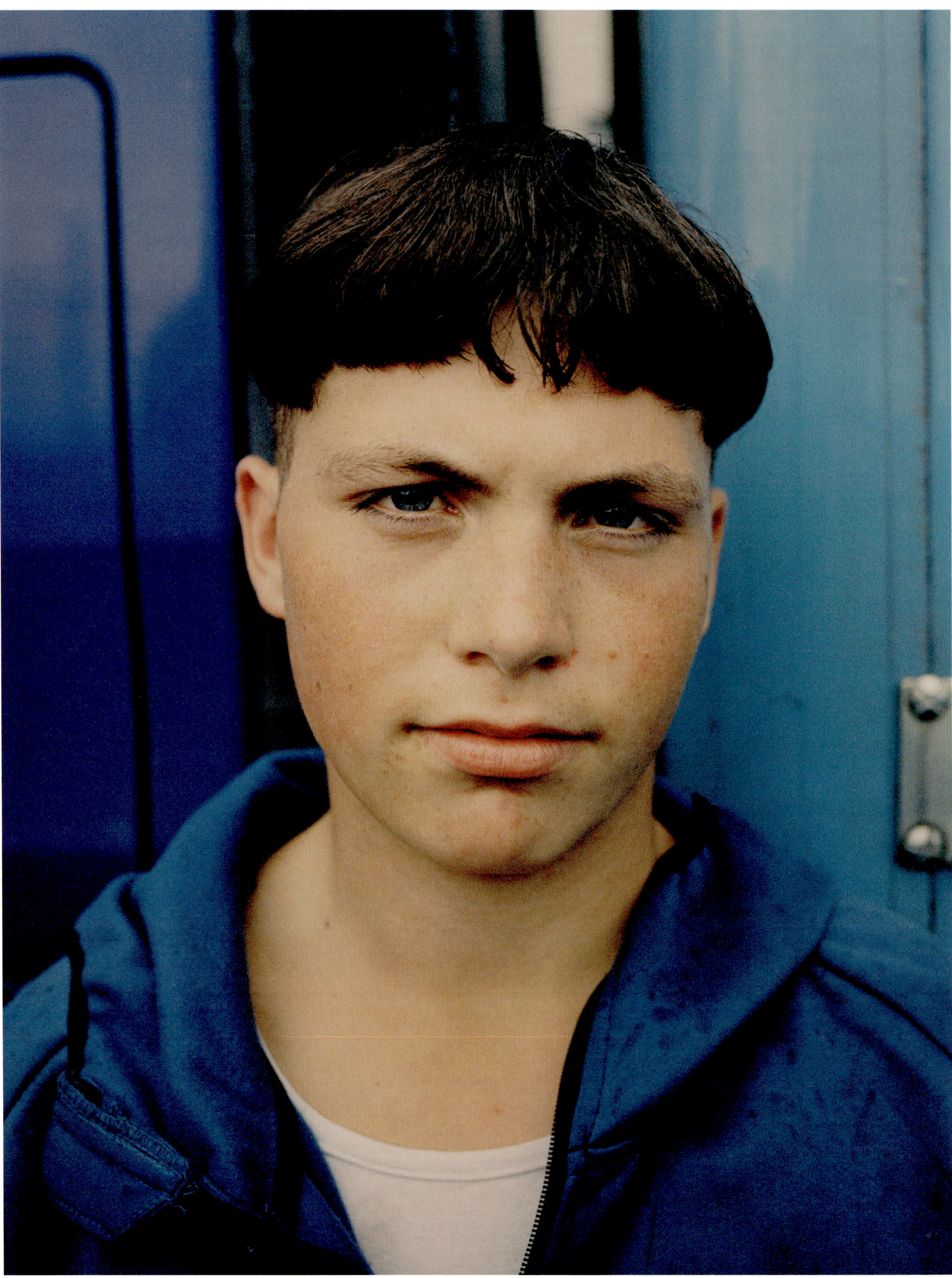

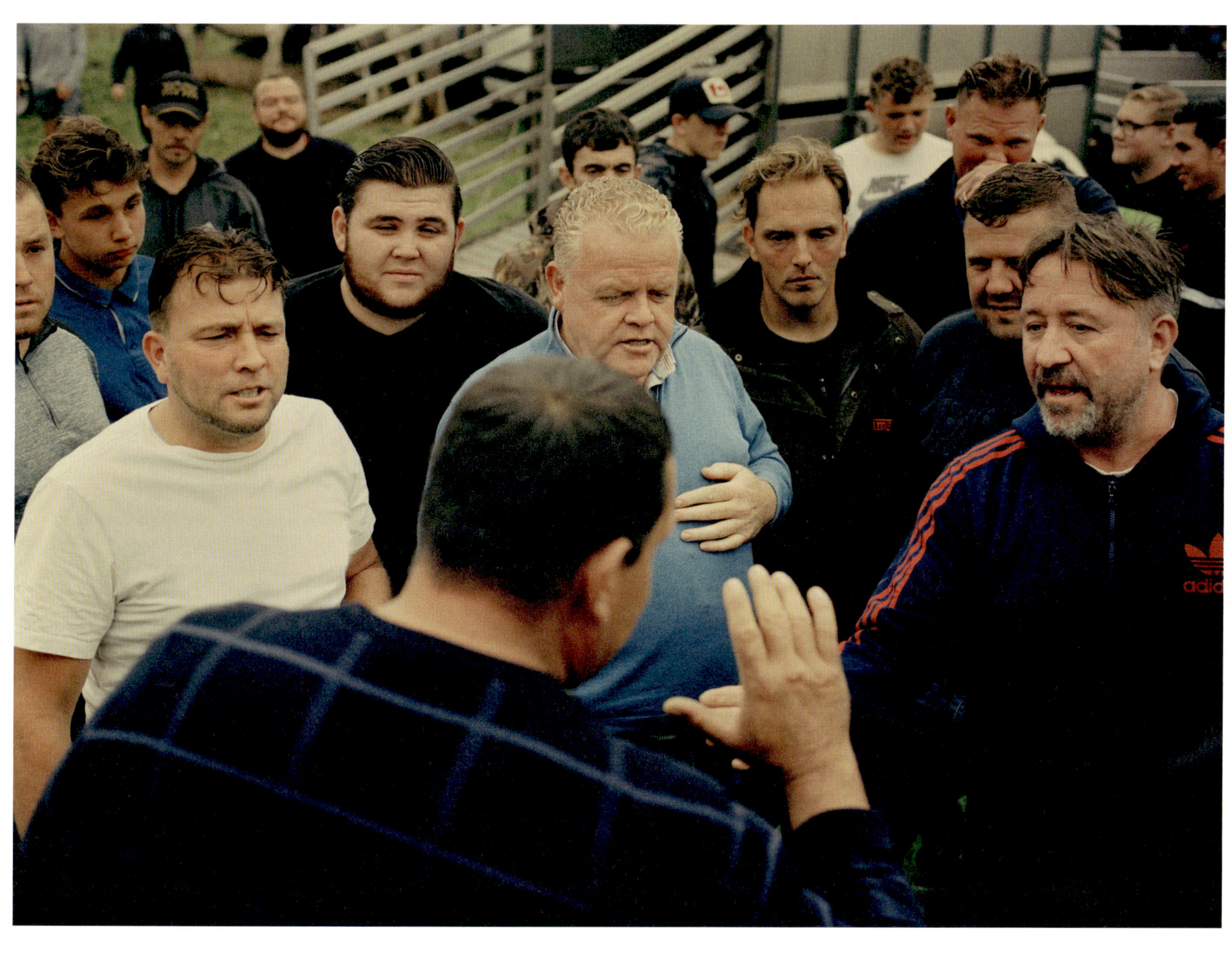

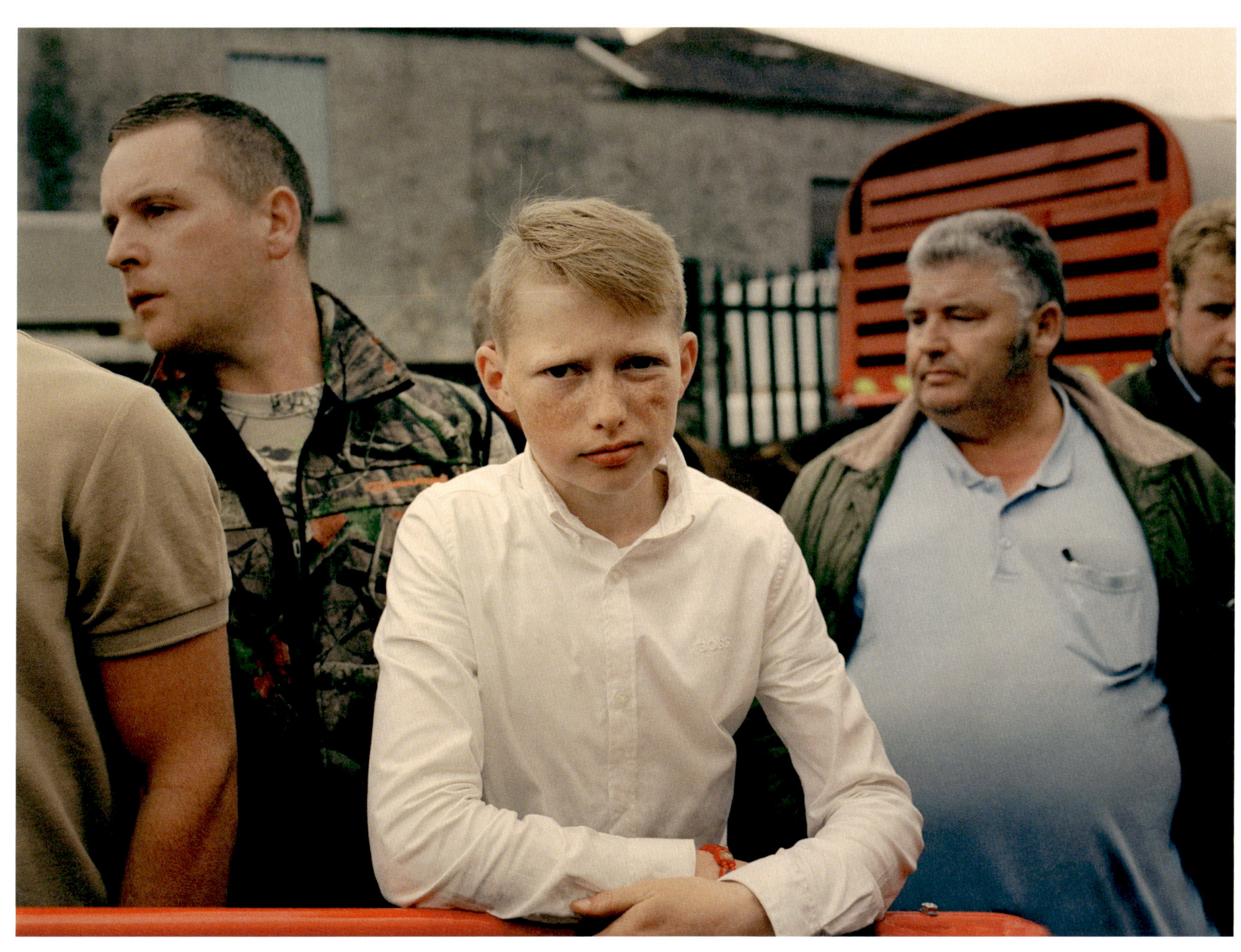

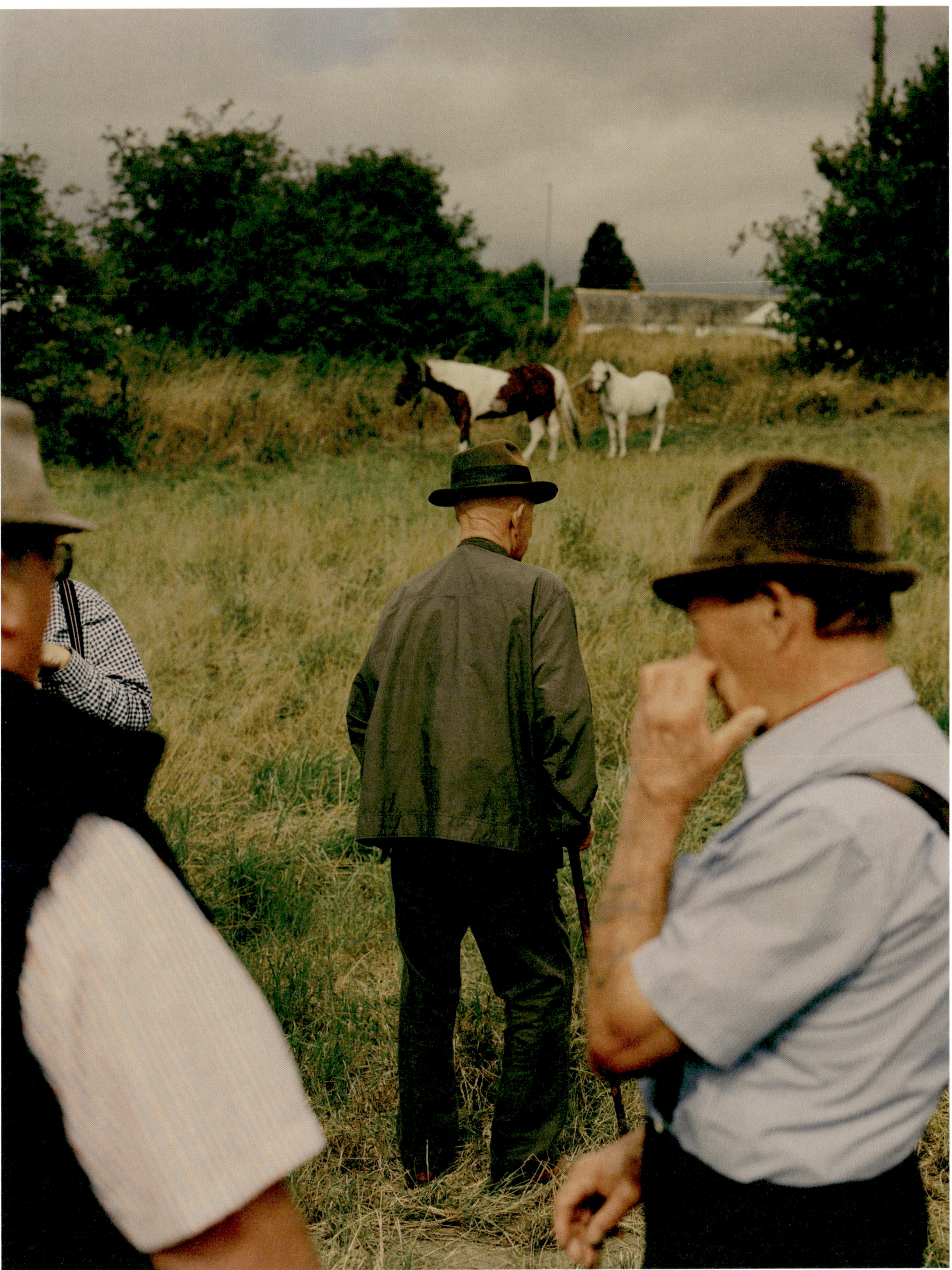

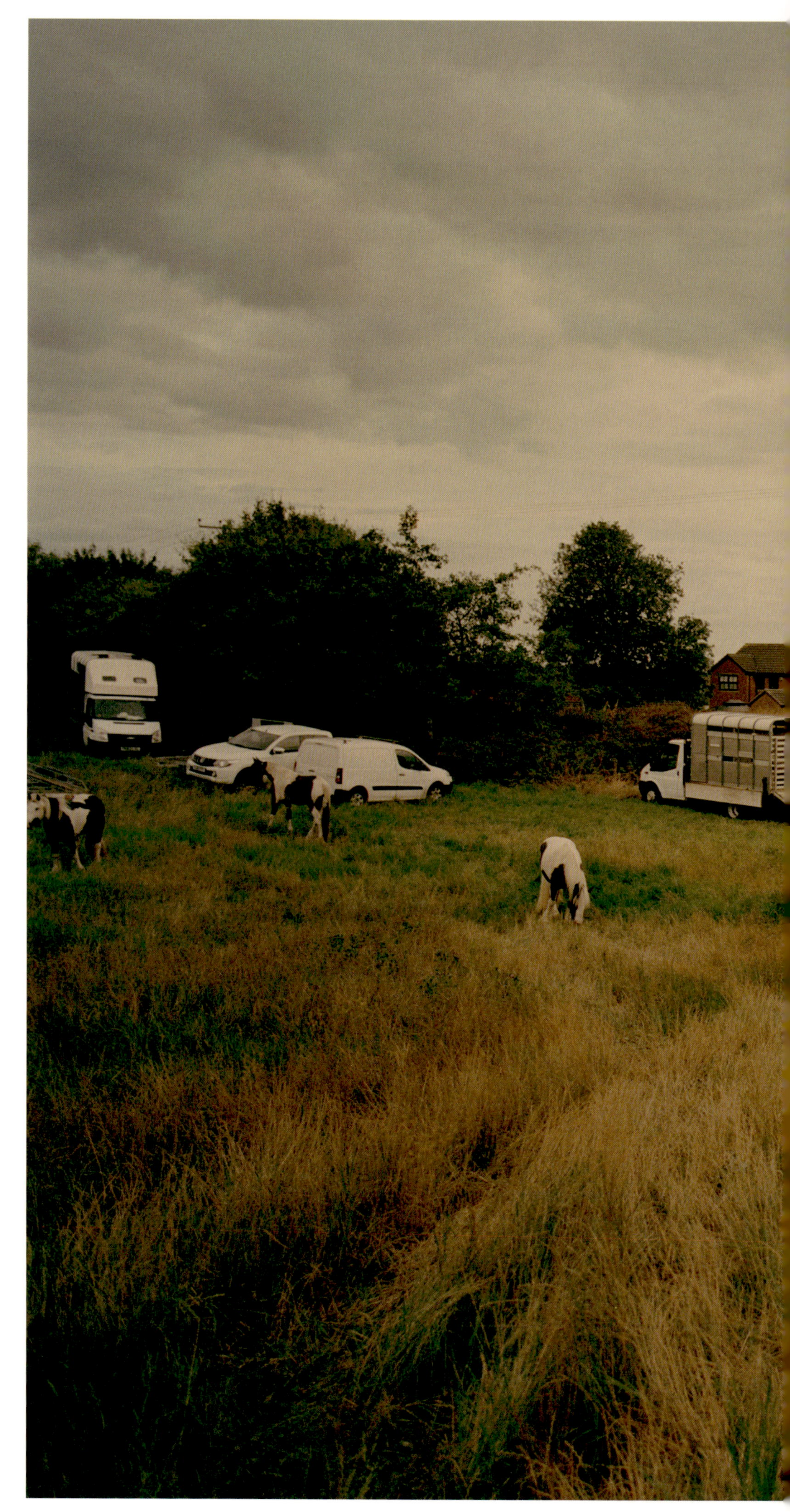

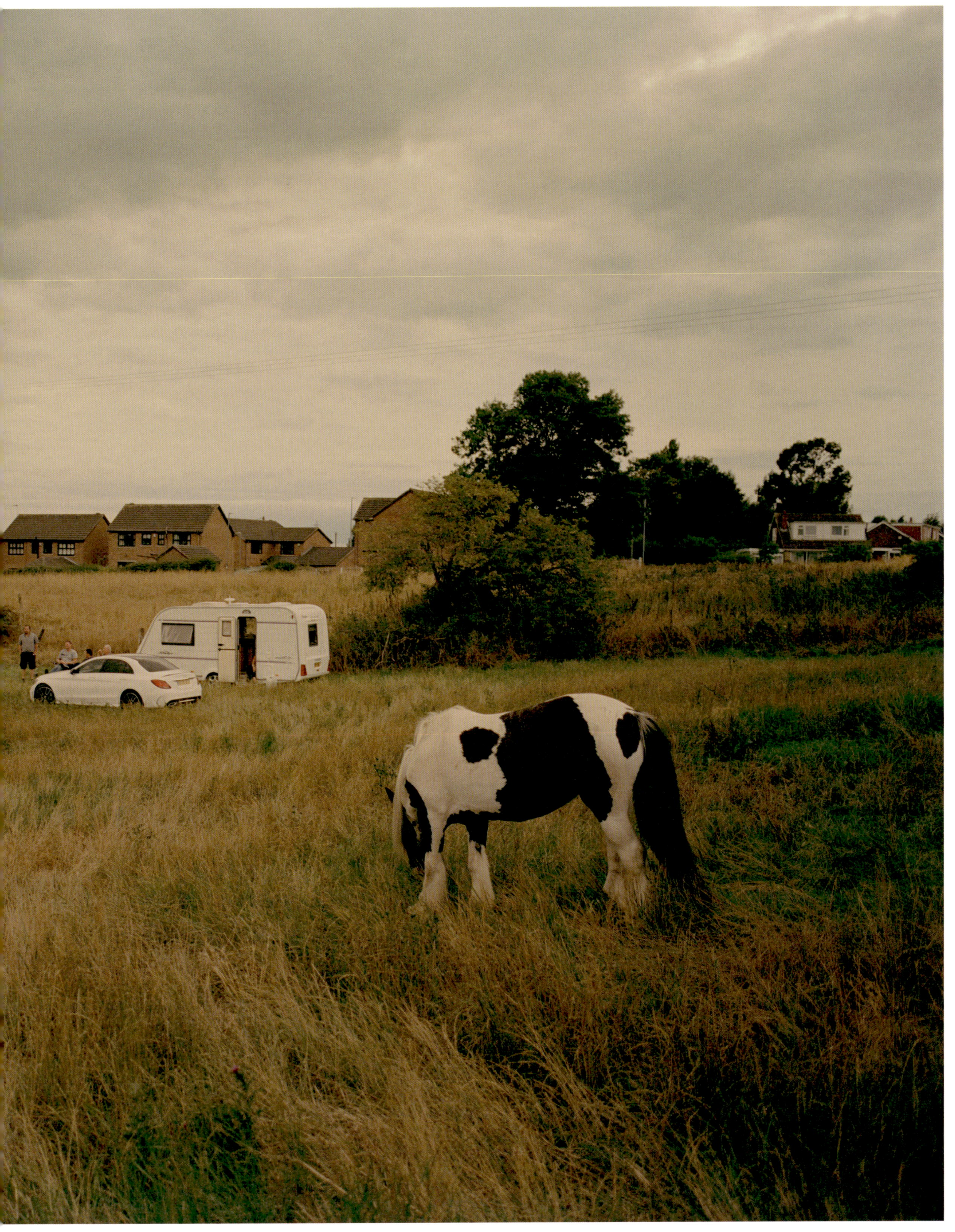

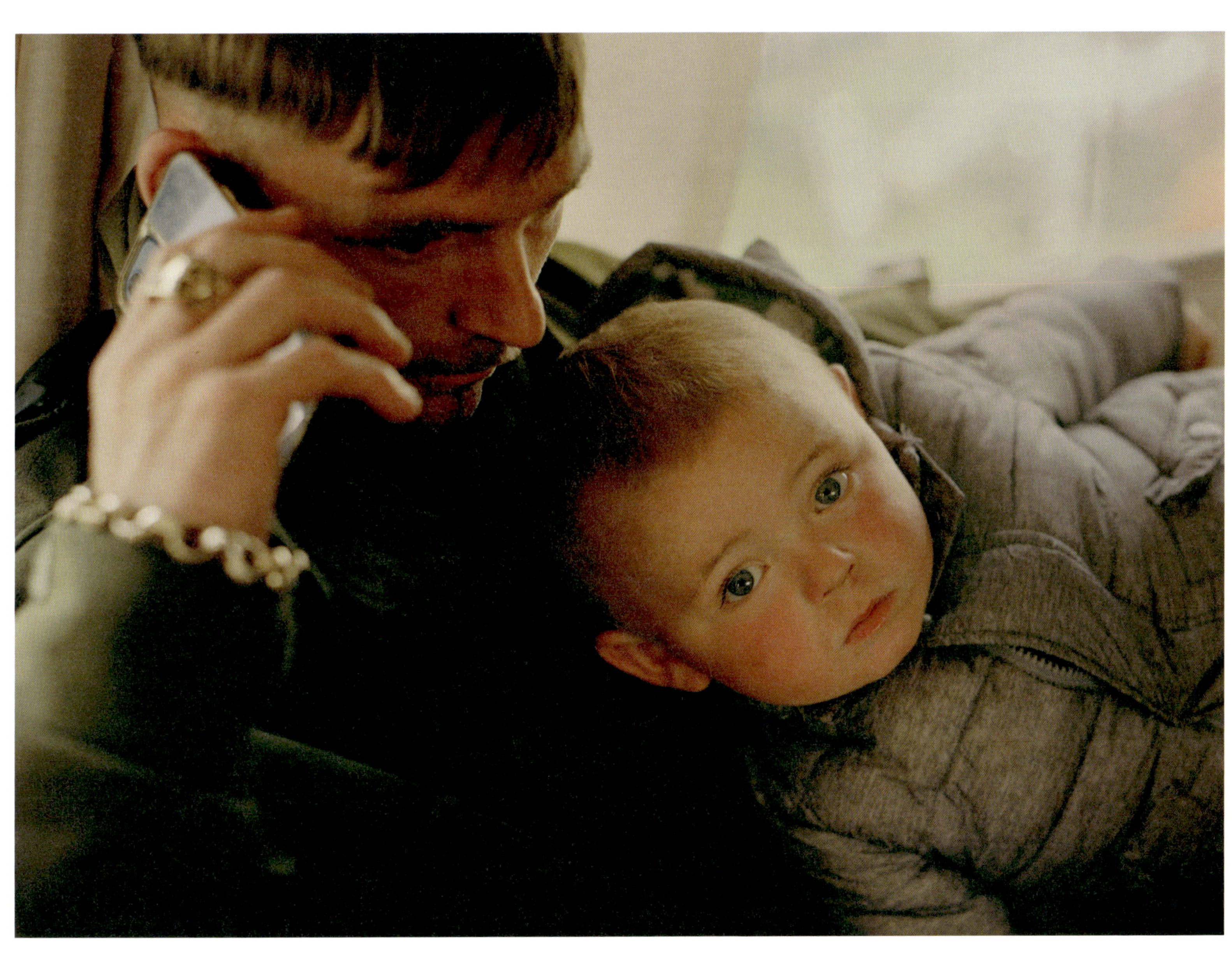

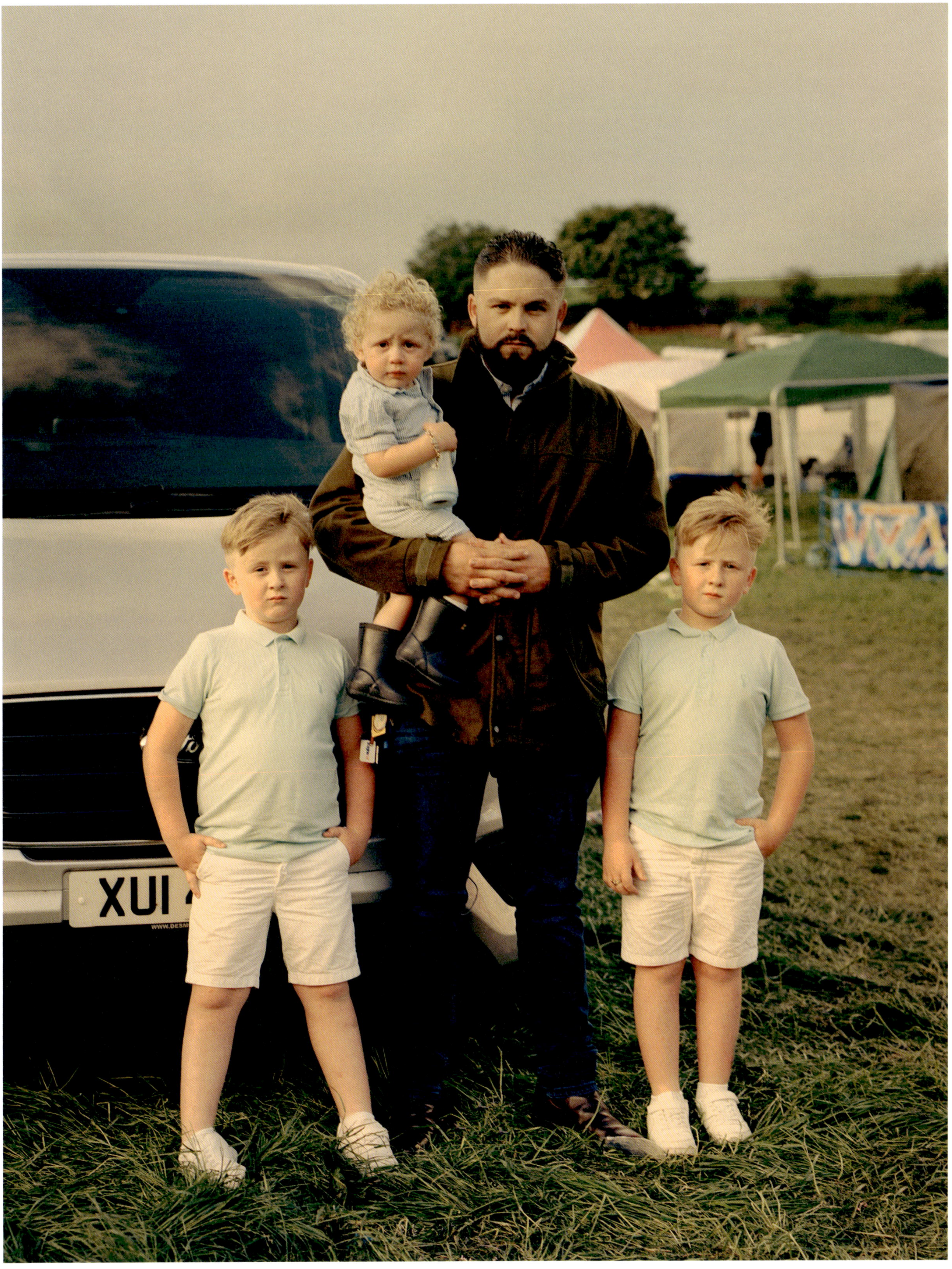
XUI

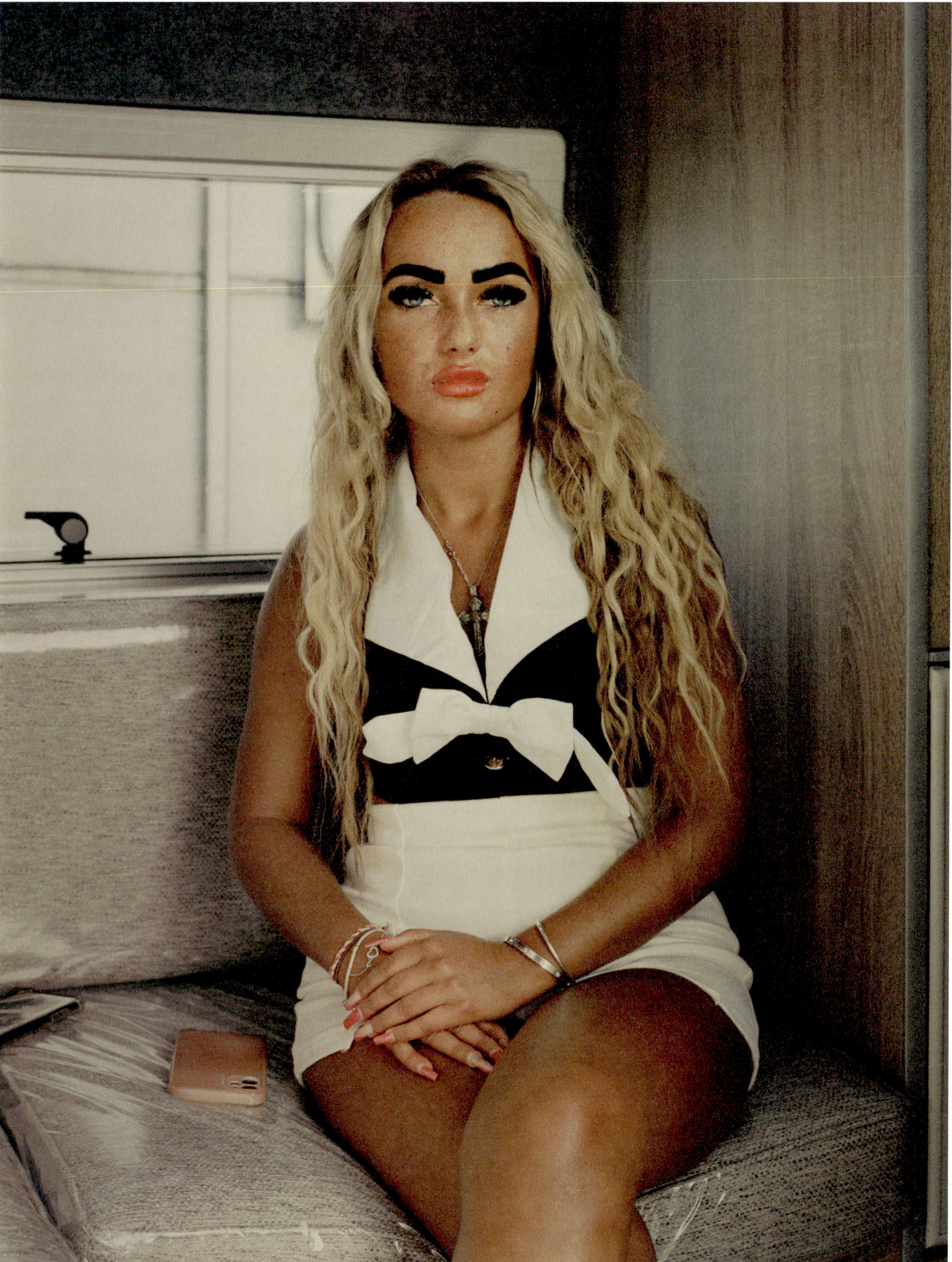

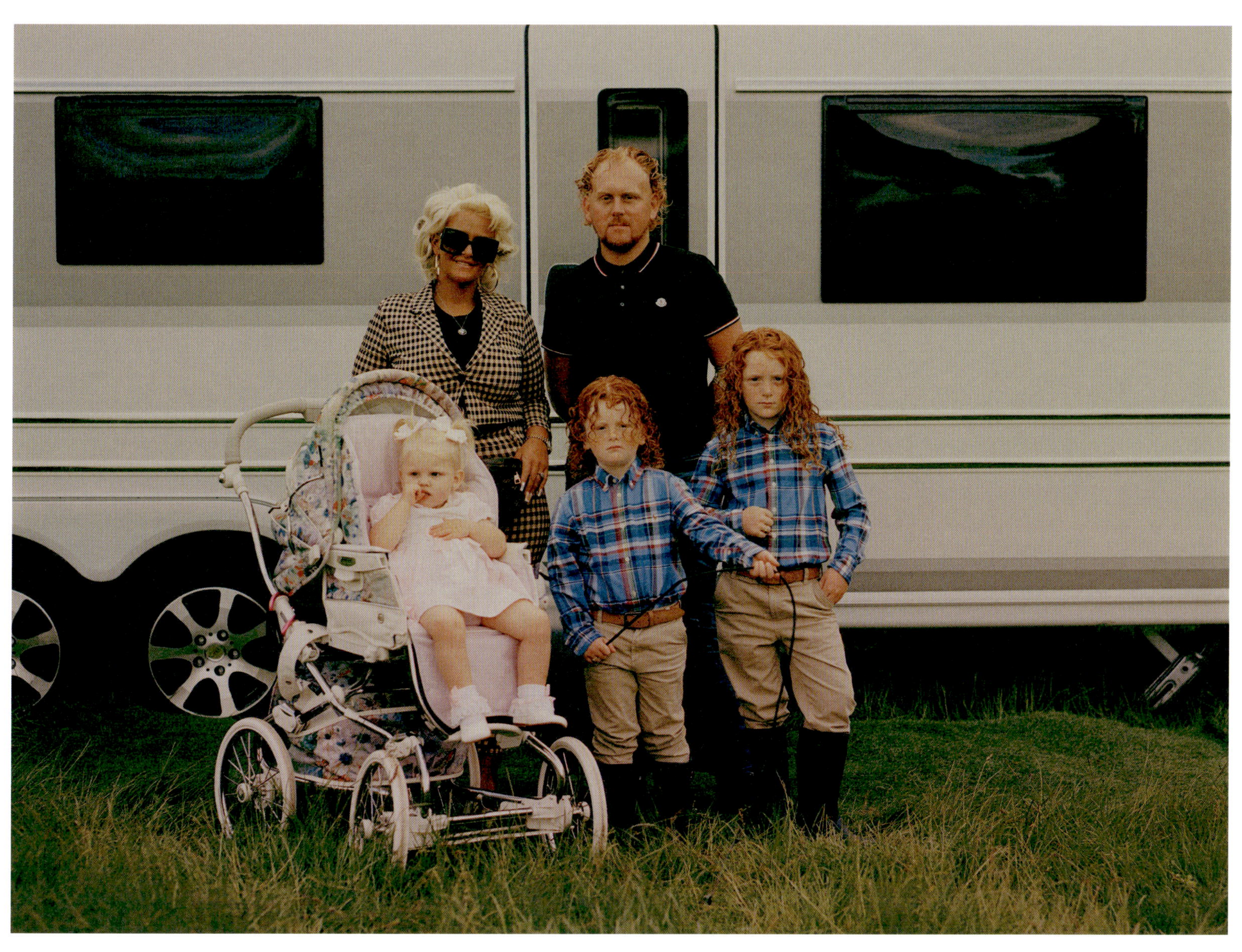

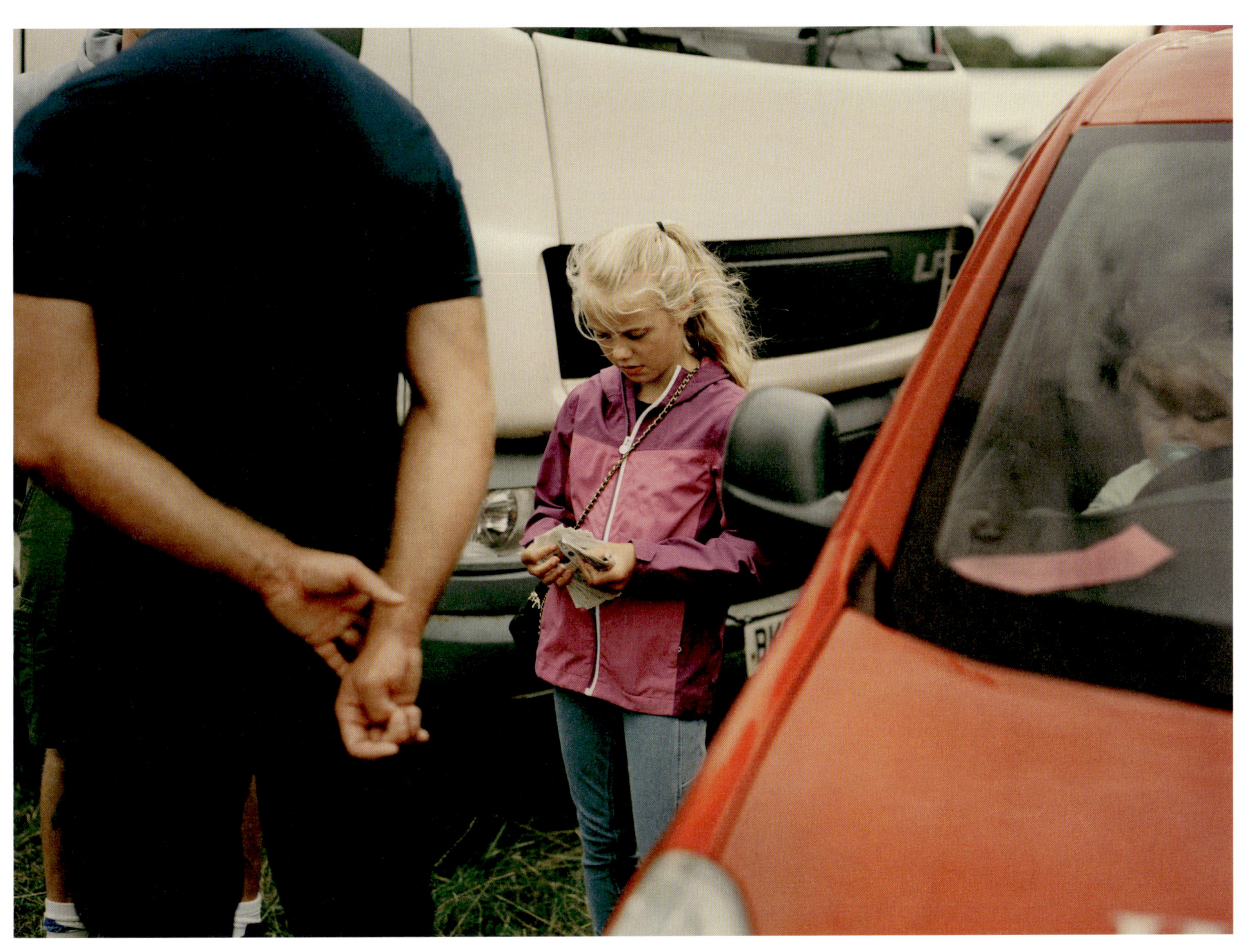

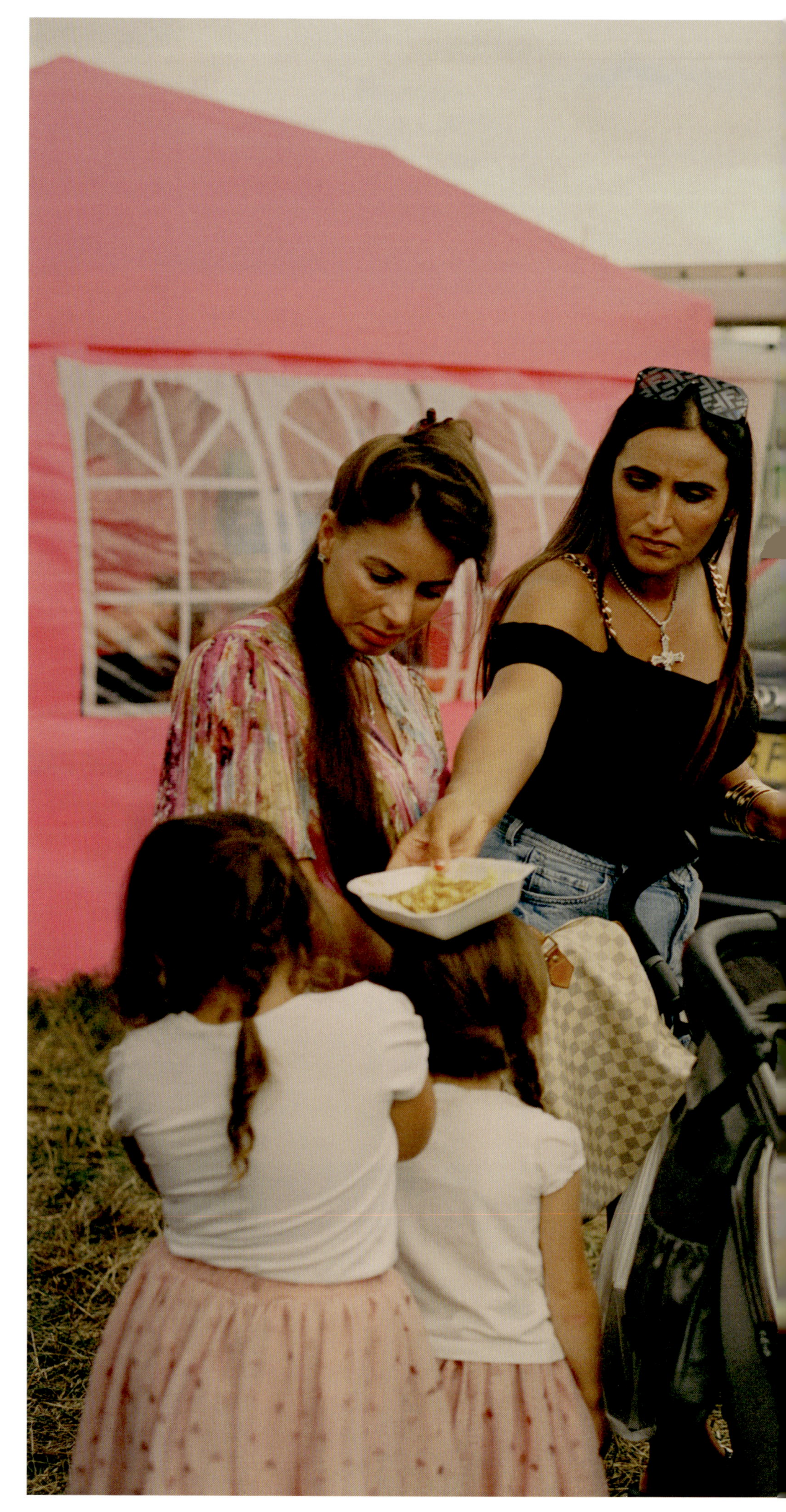

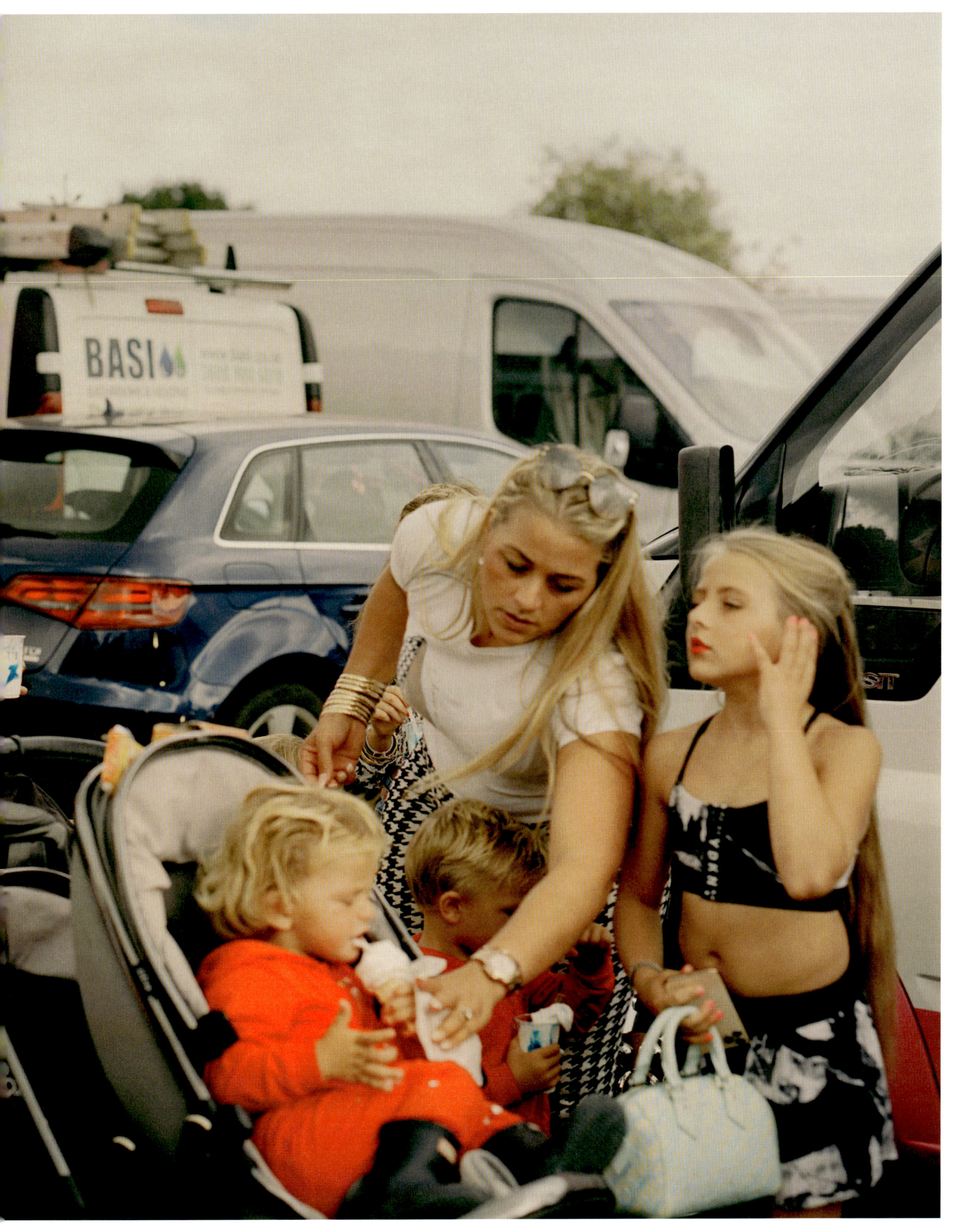
BASI

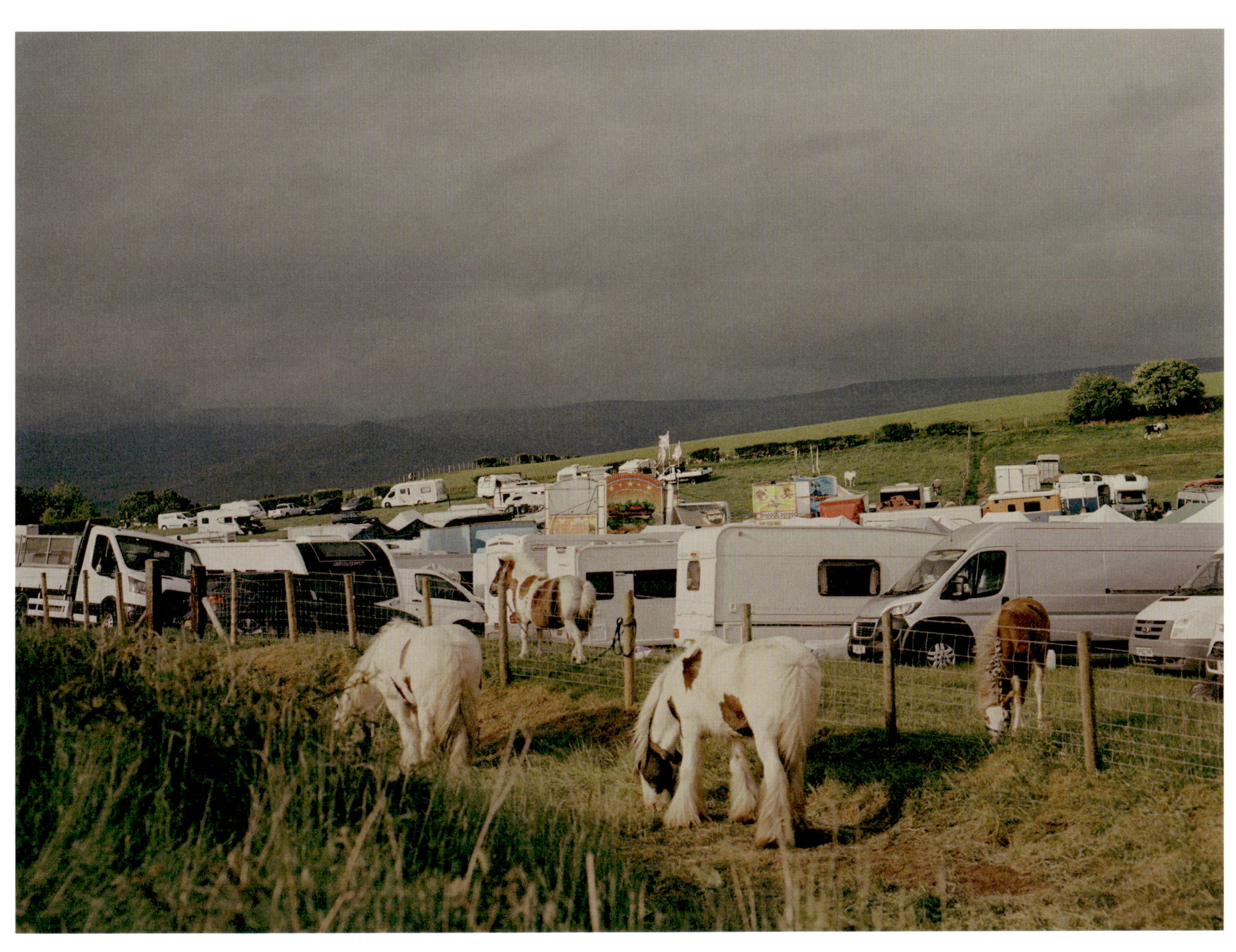

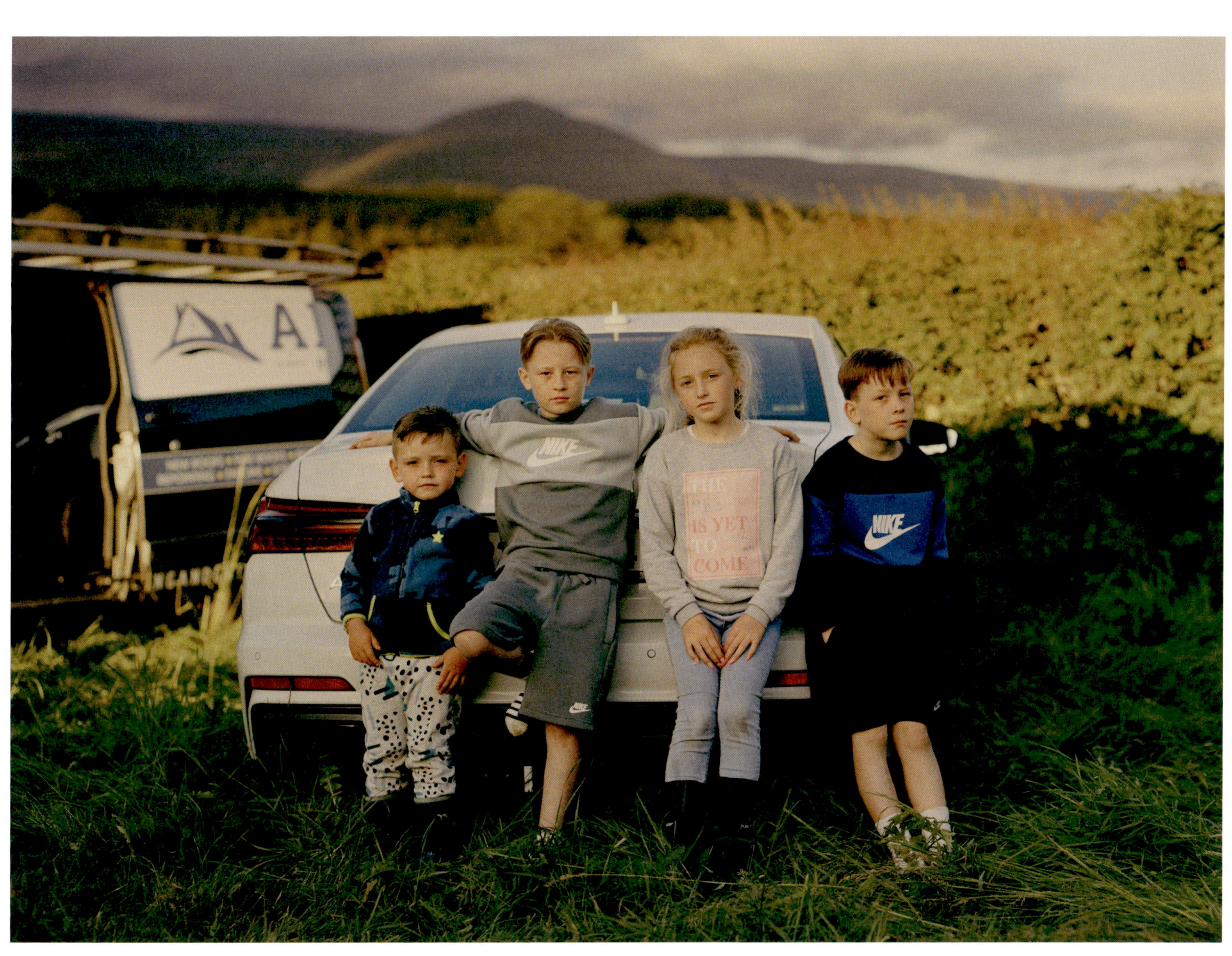
NIKE
THE
IS YET
TO
COME
NIKE

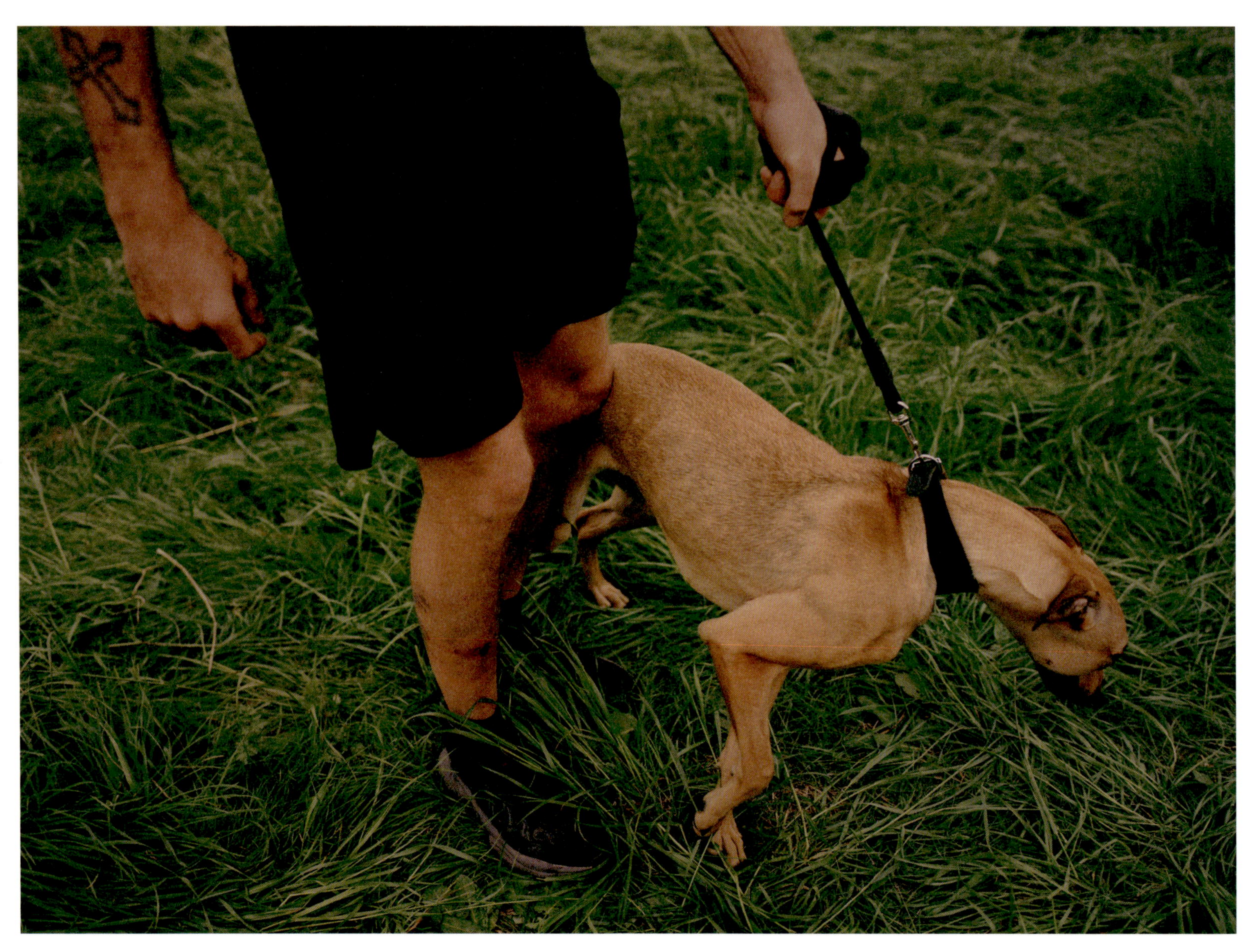

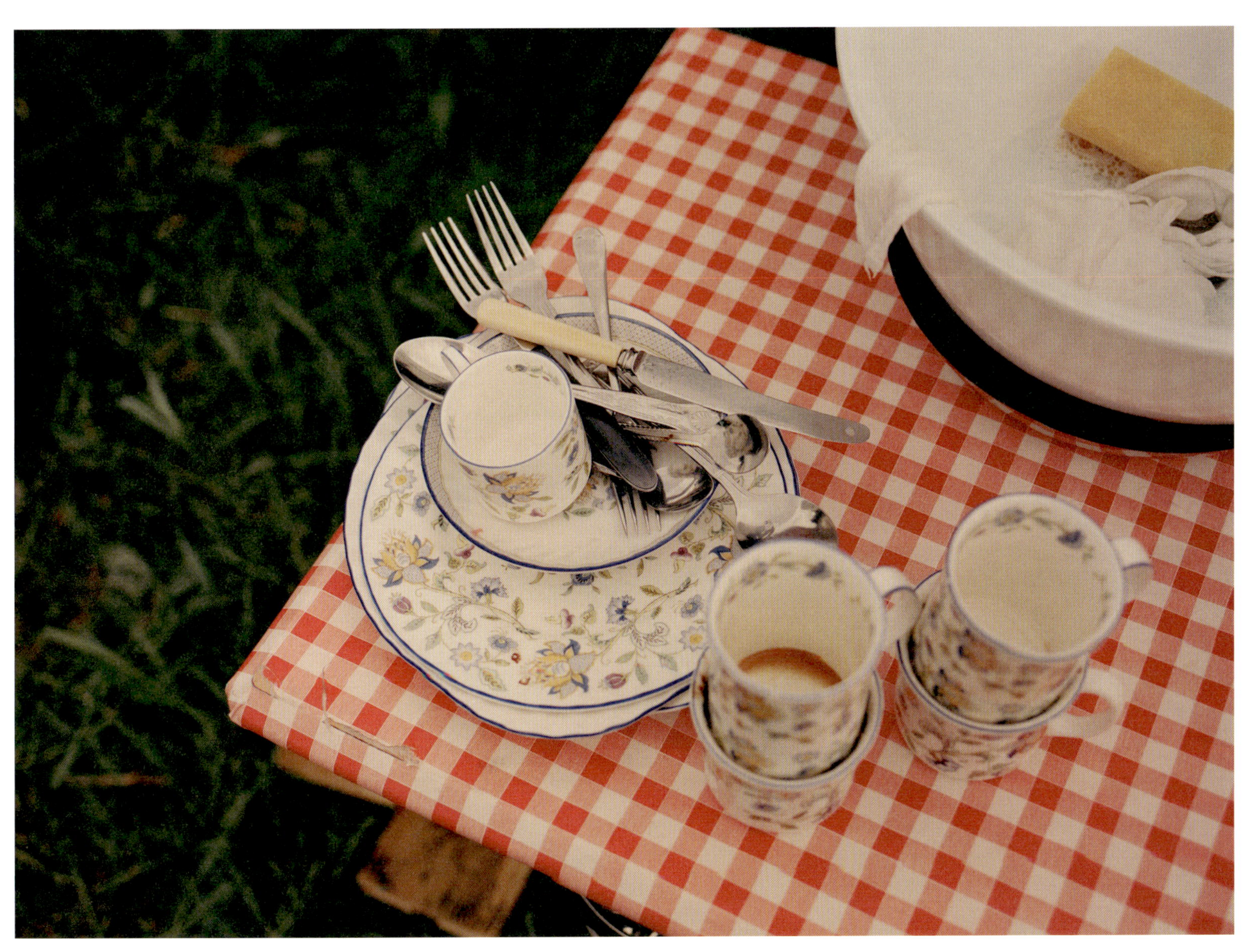

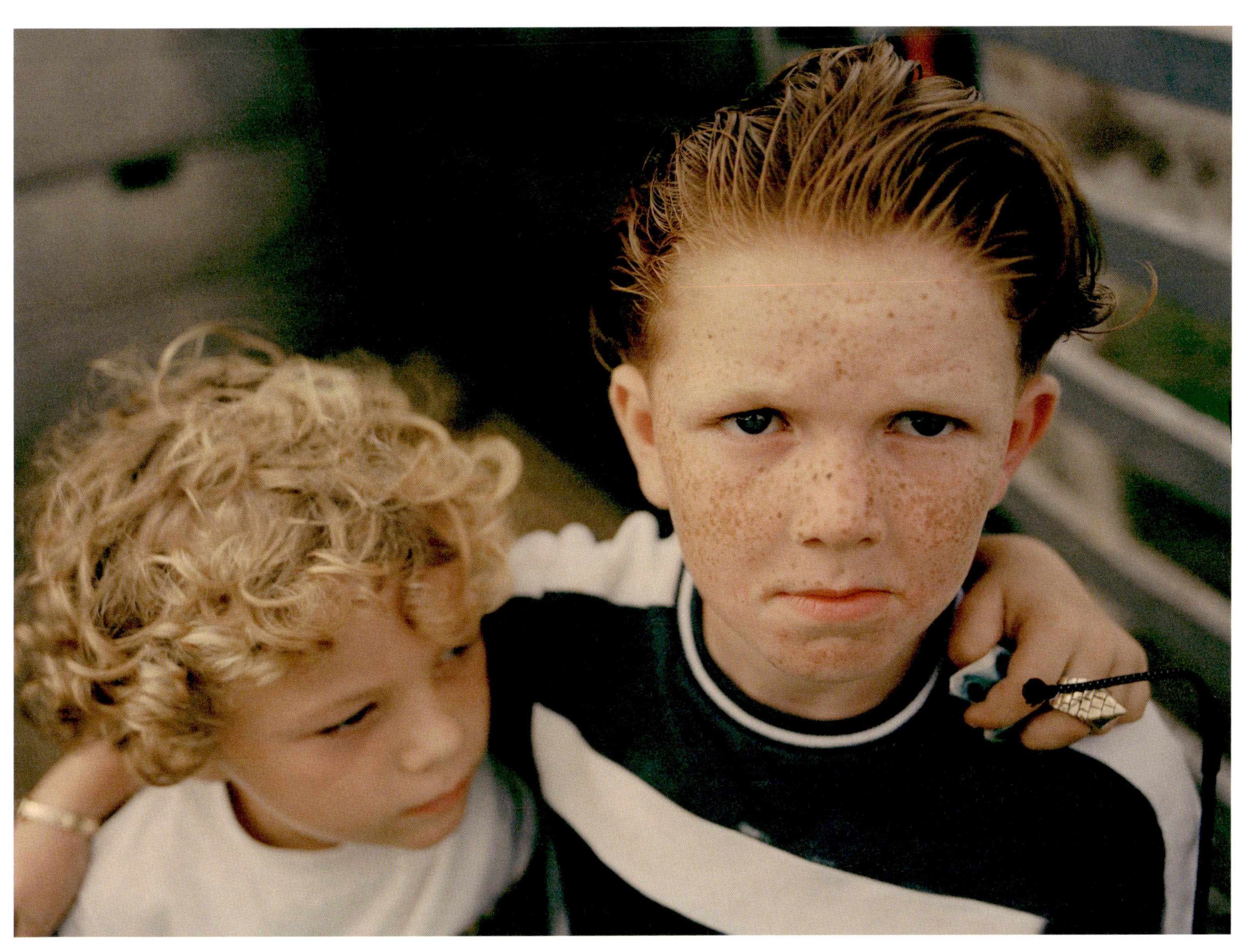

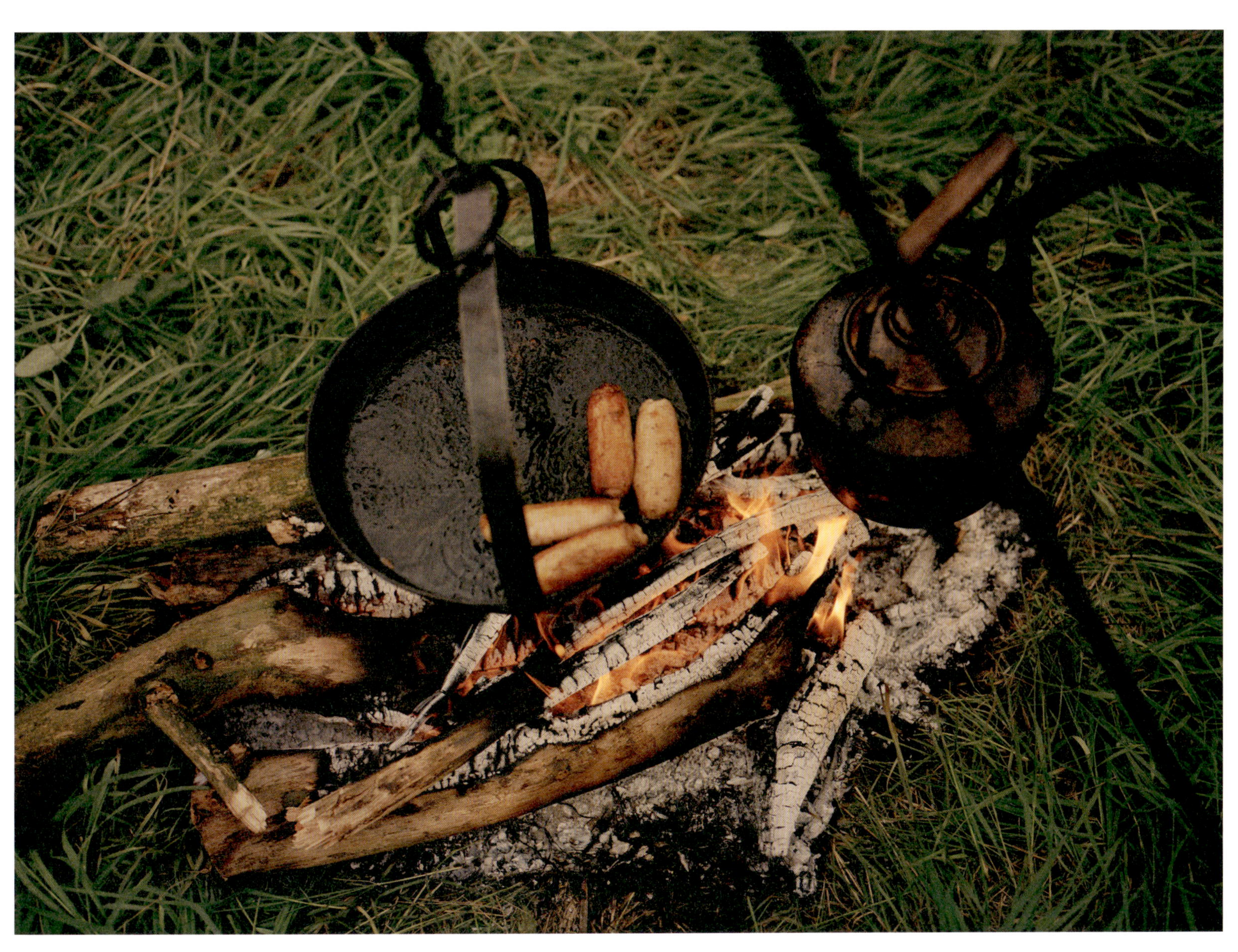

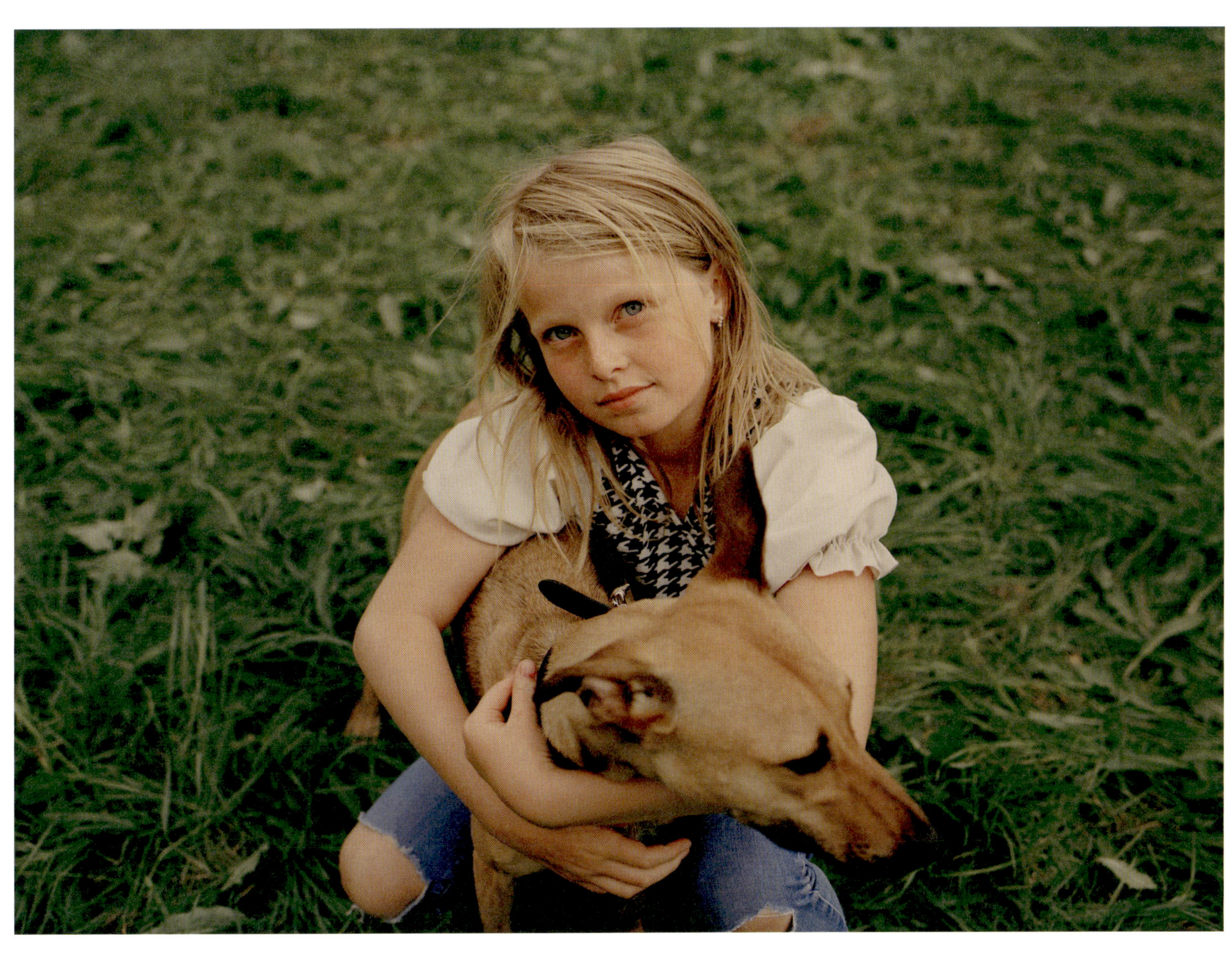

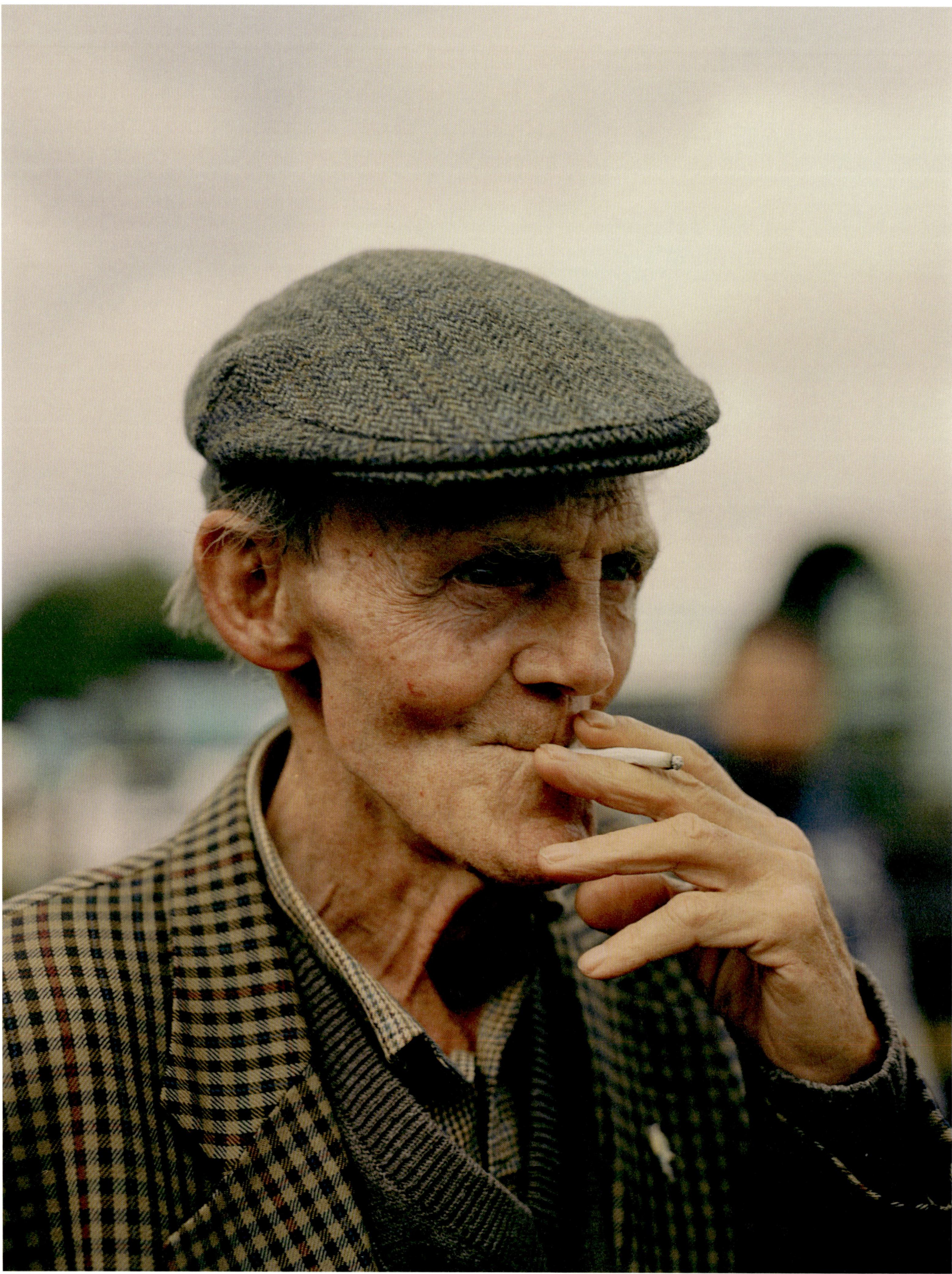

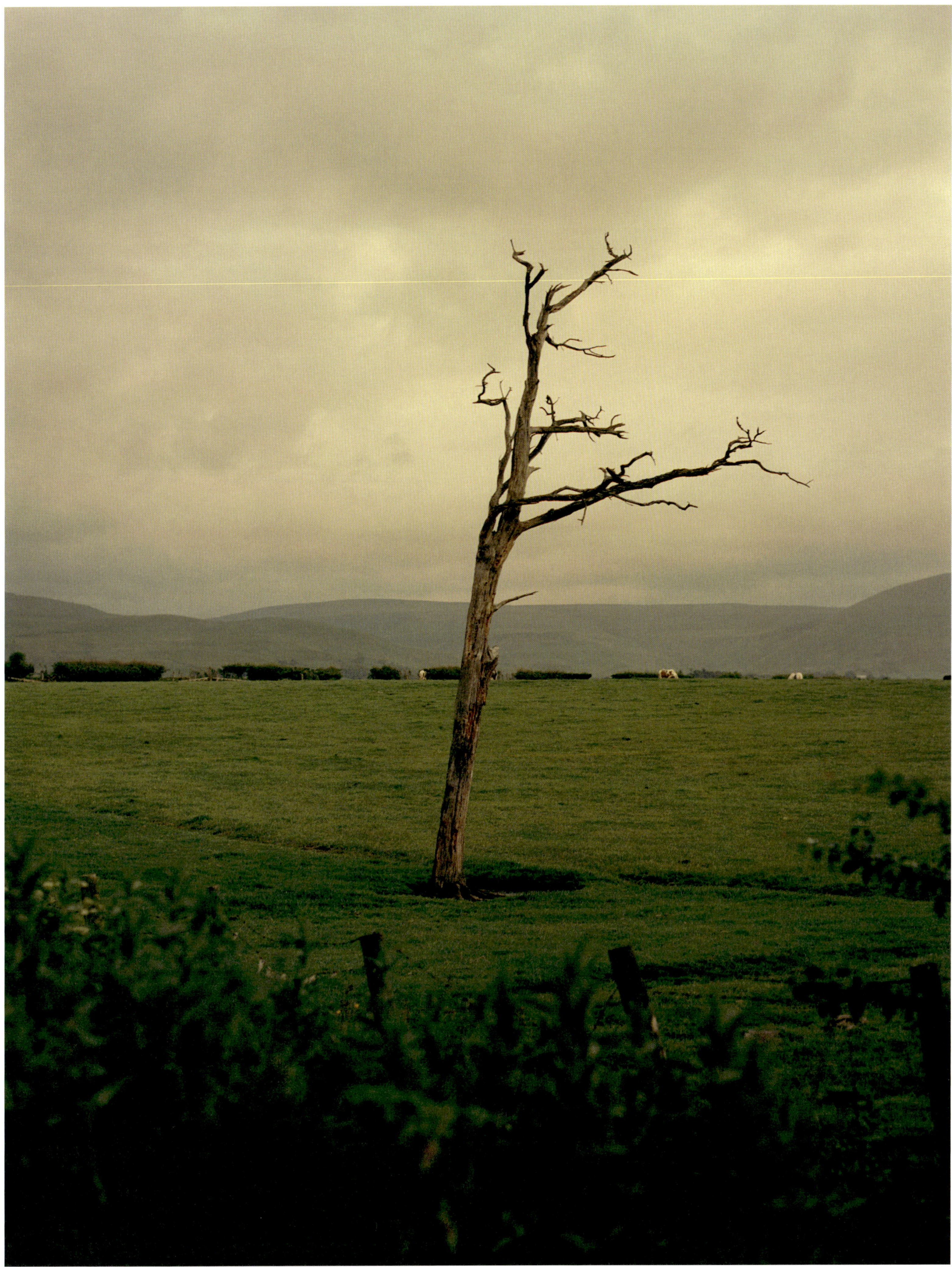

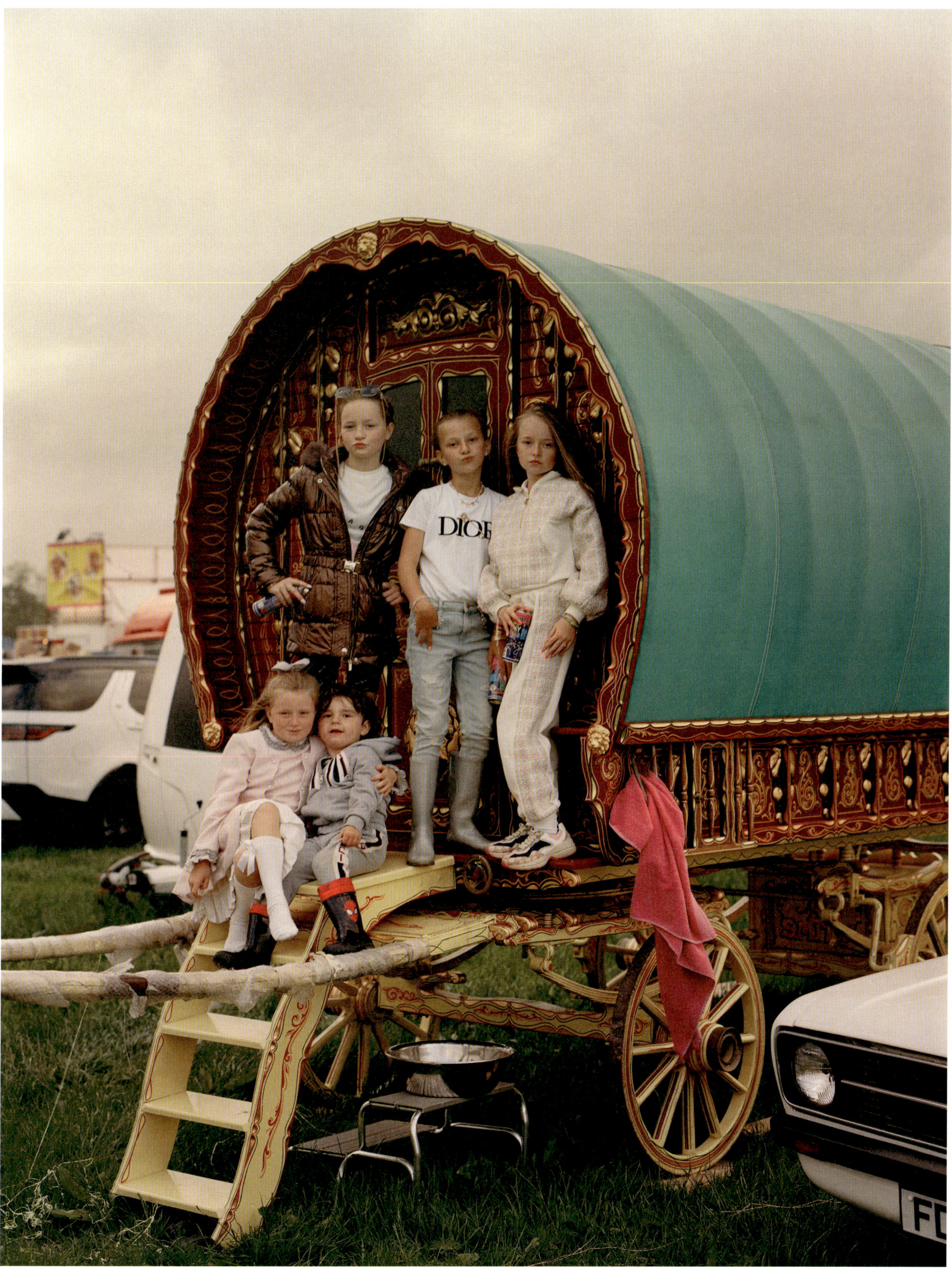
DIOR

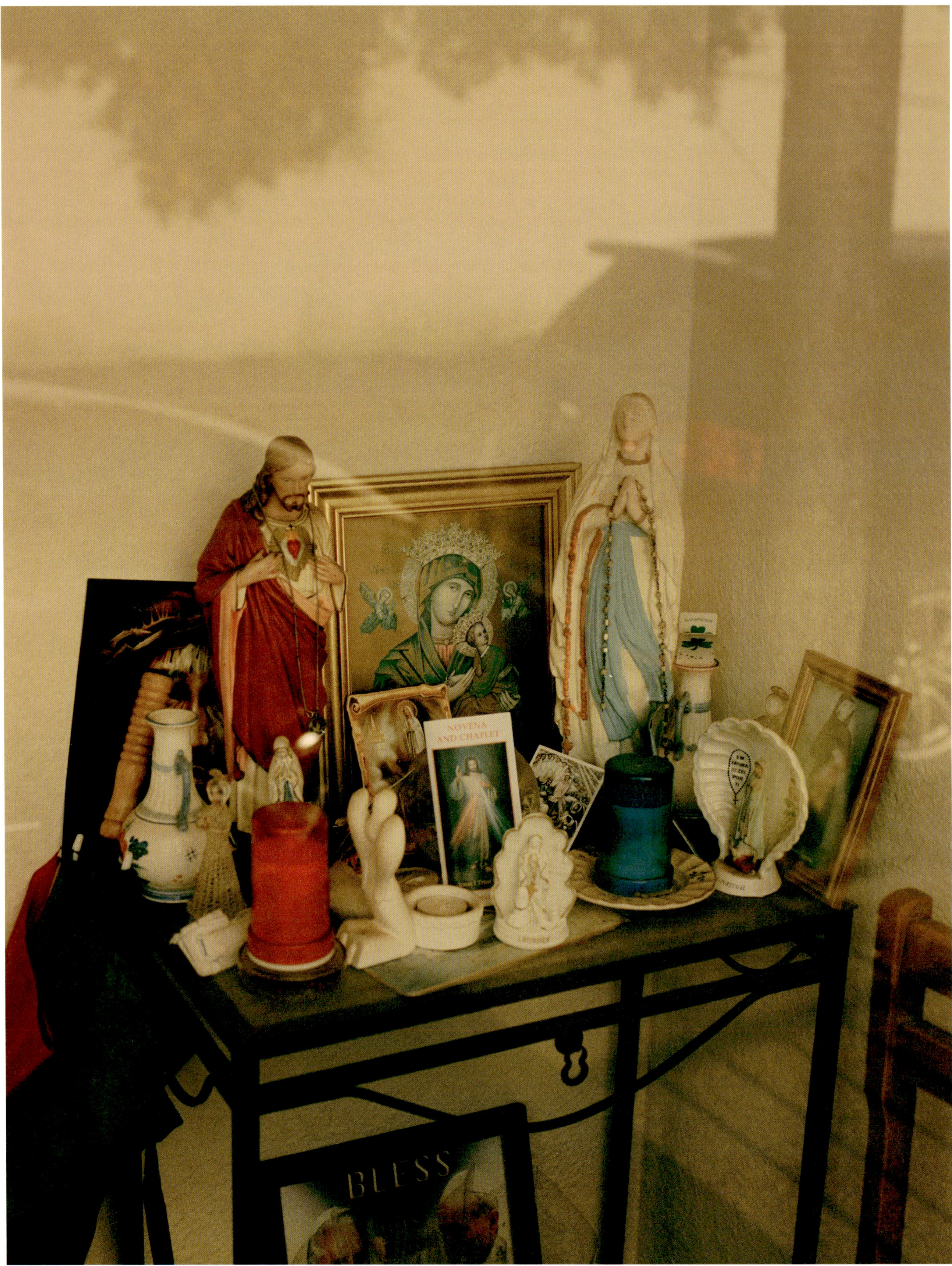
NOVENA
AND CHAPLET
BLESS

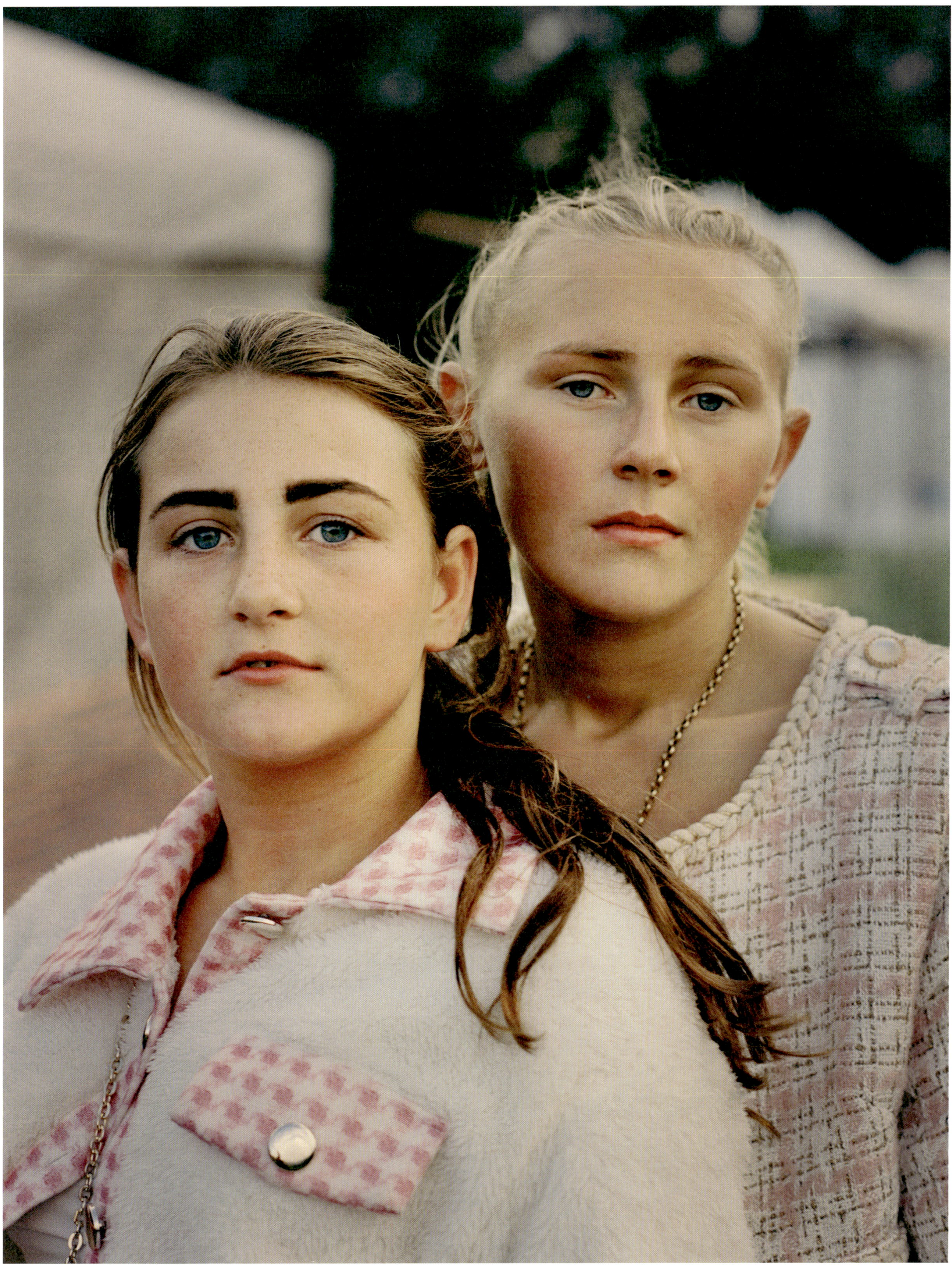

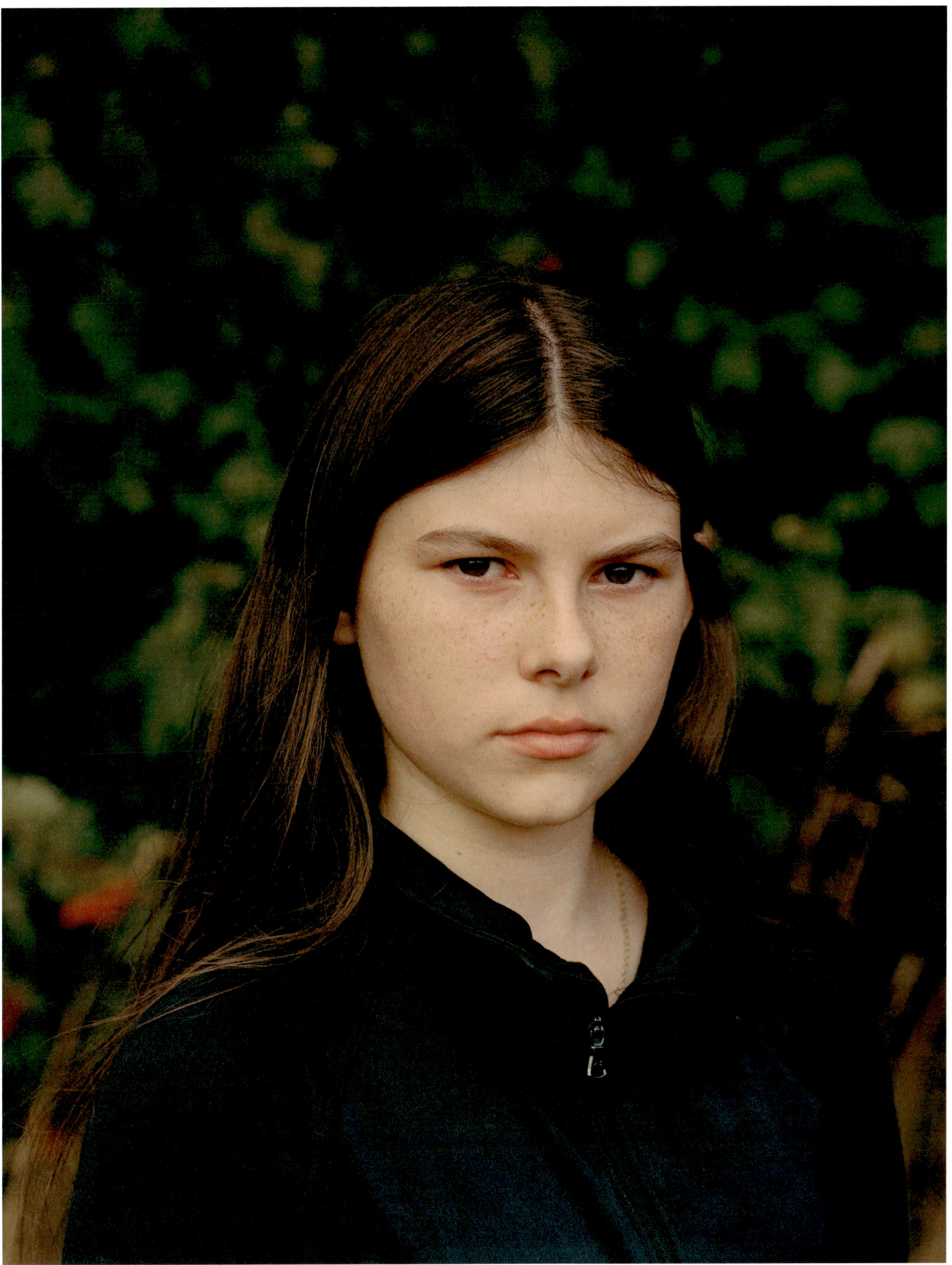

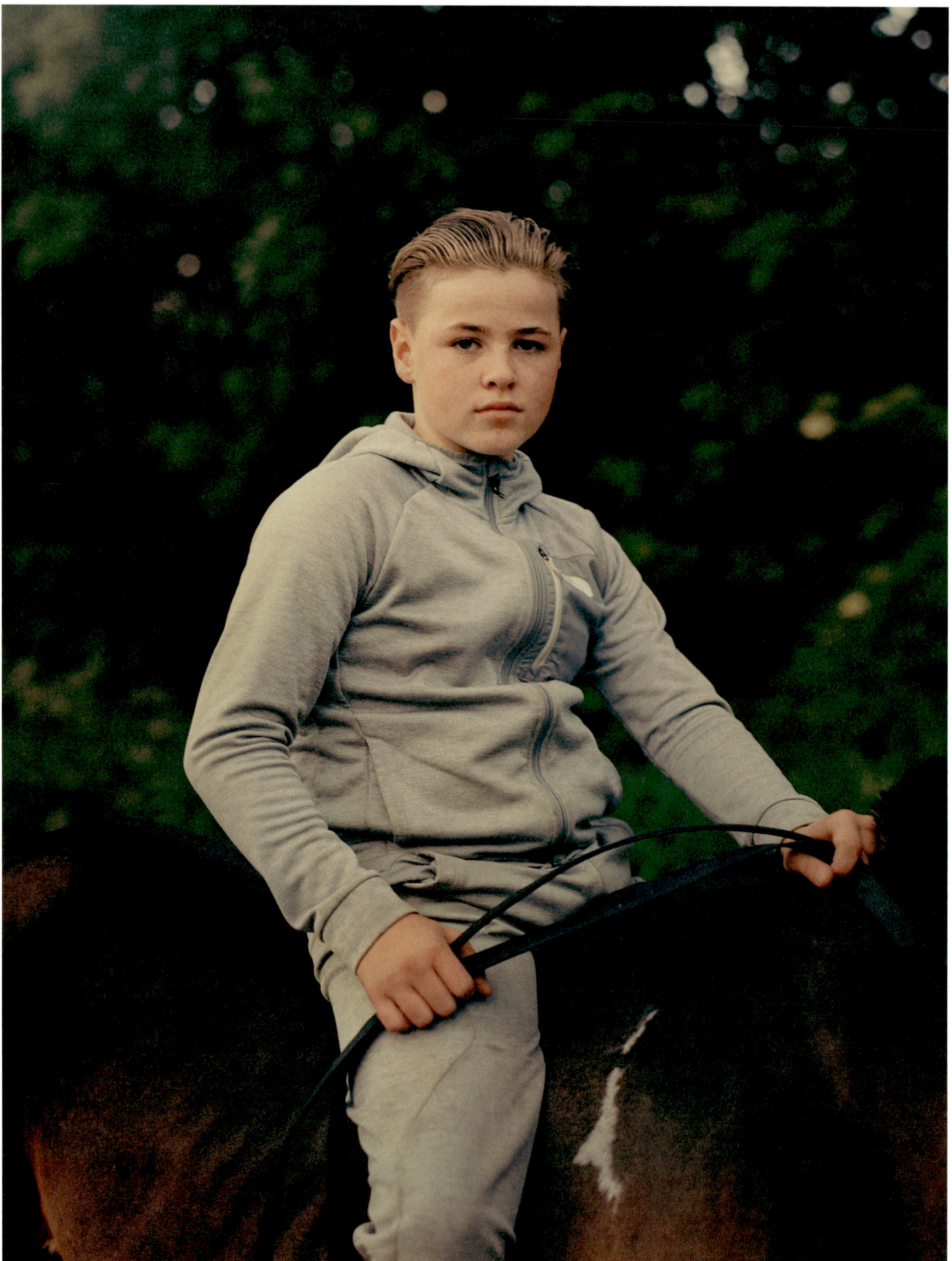

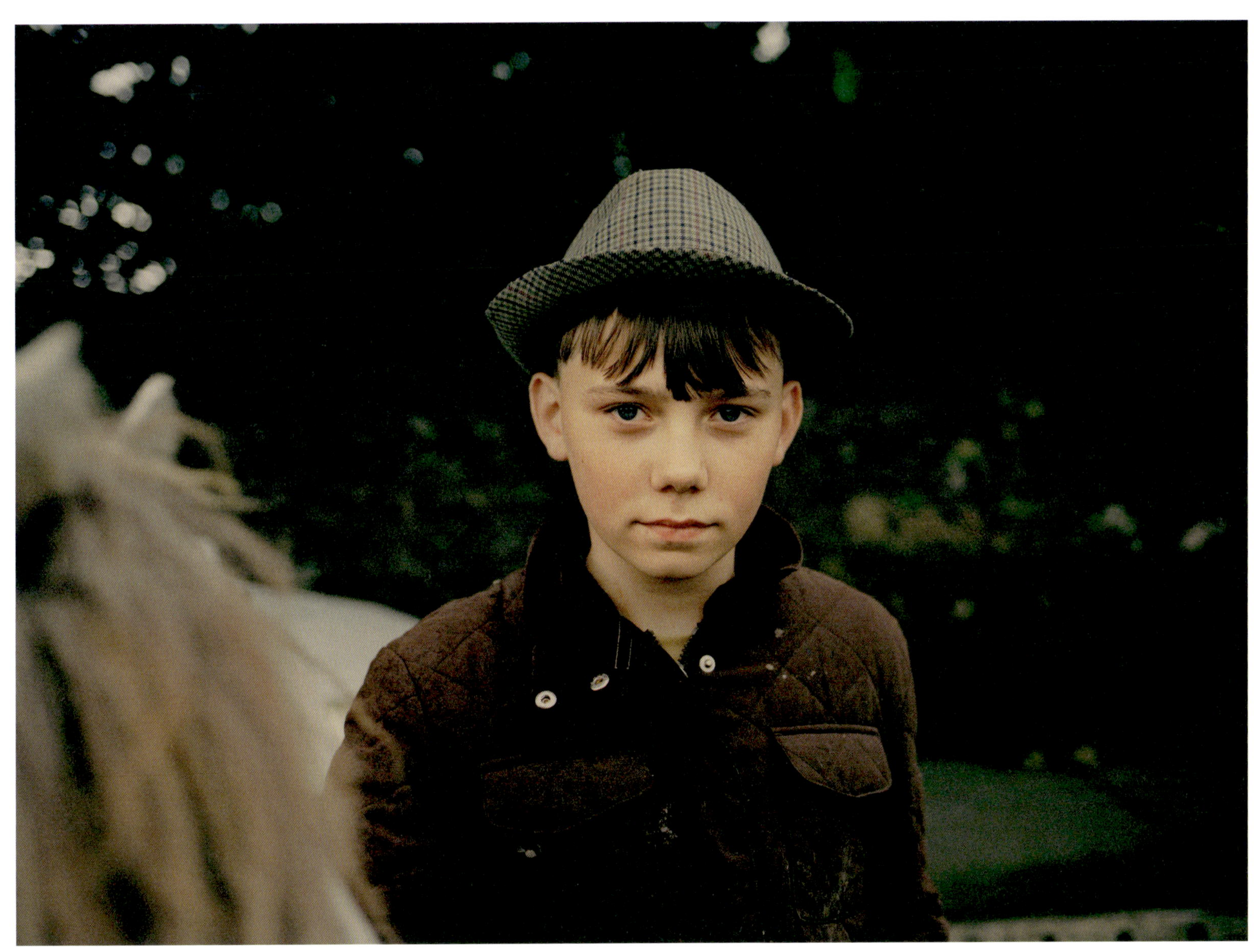

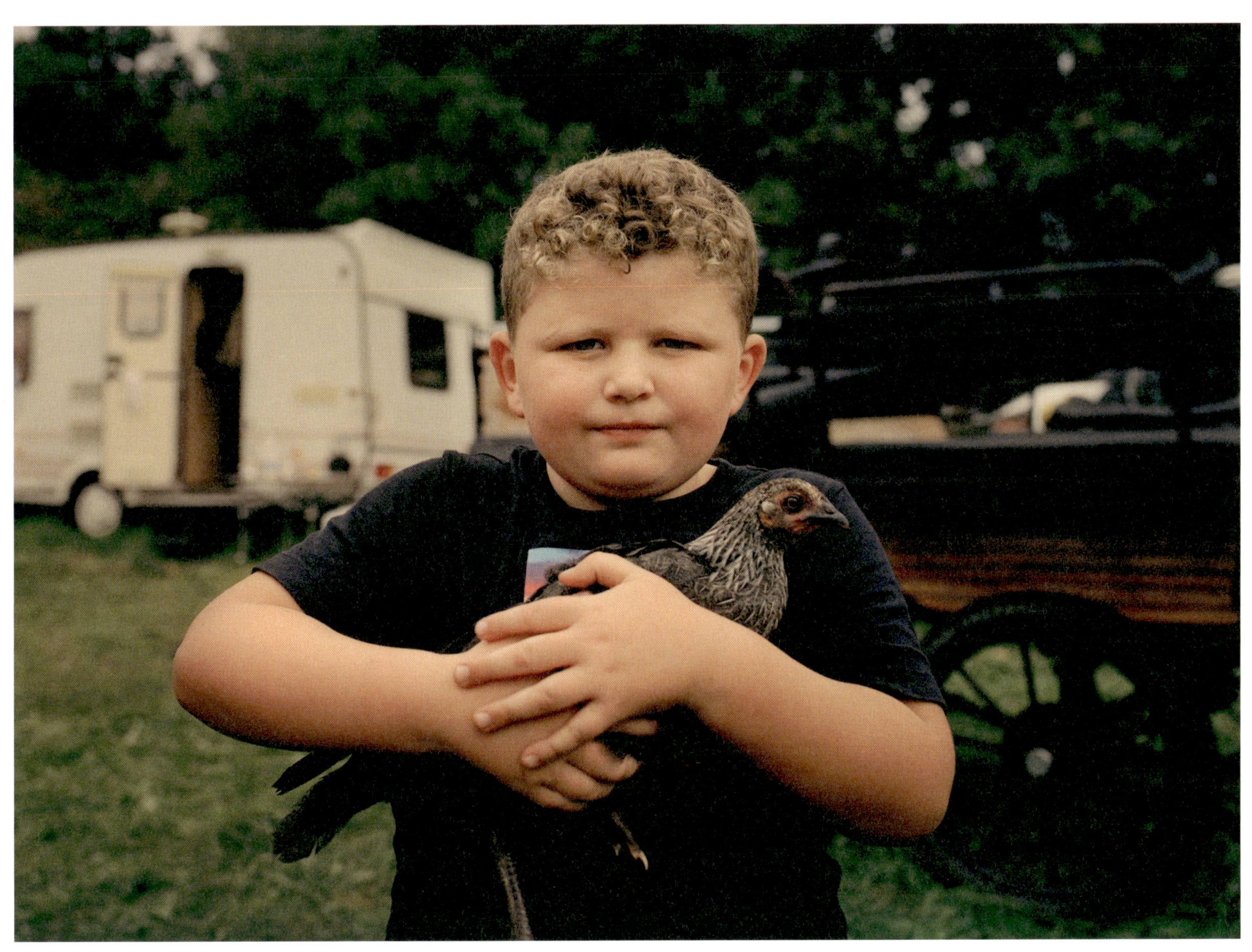

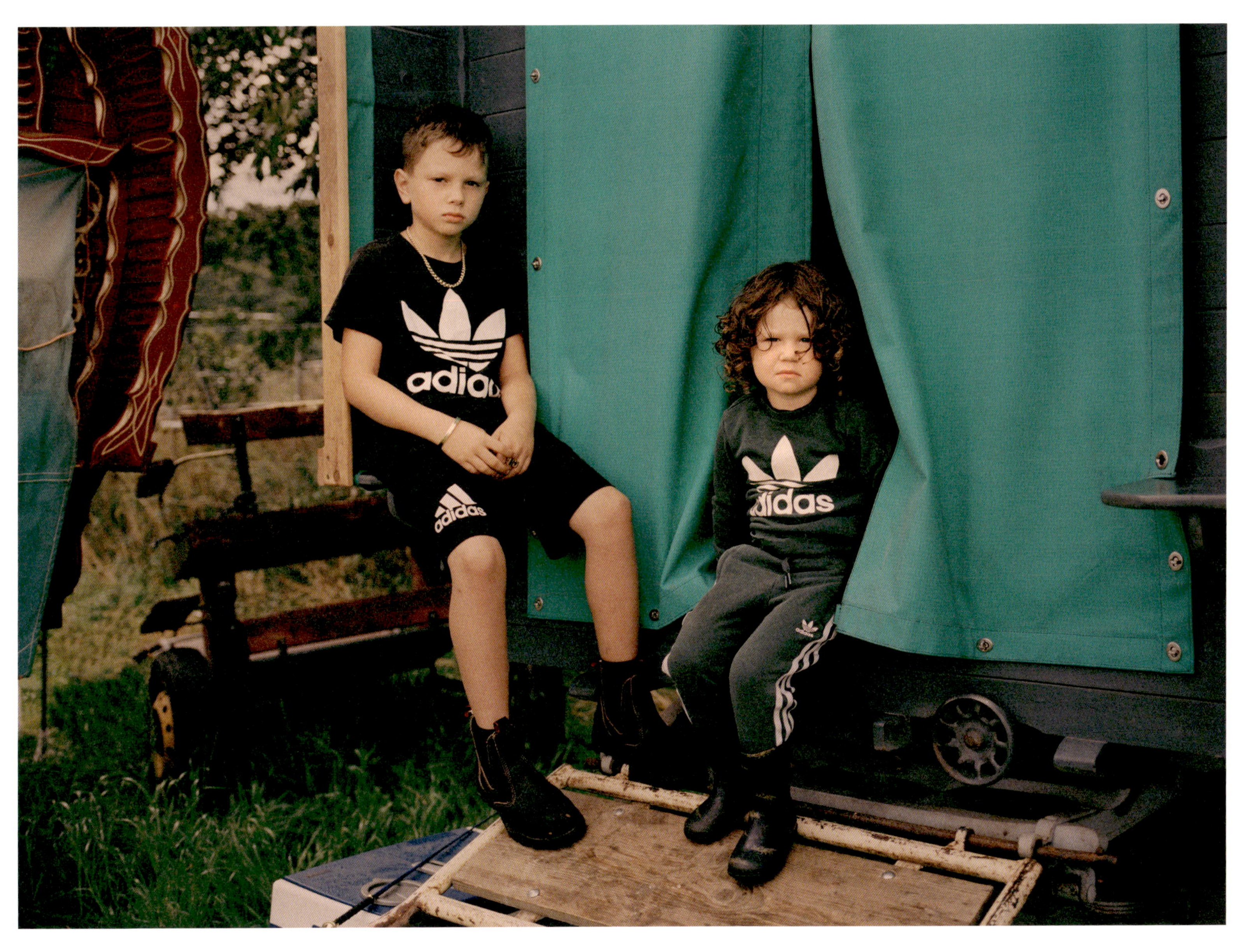
adidas
adidas

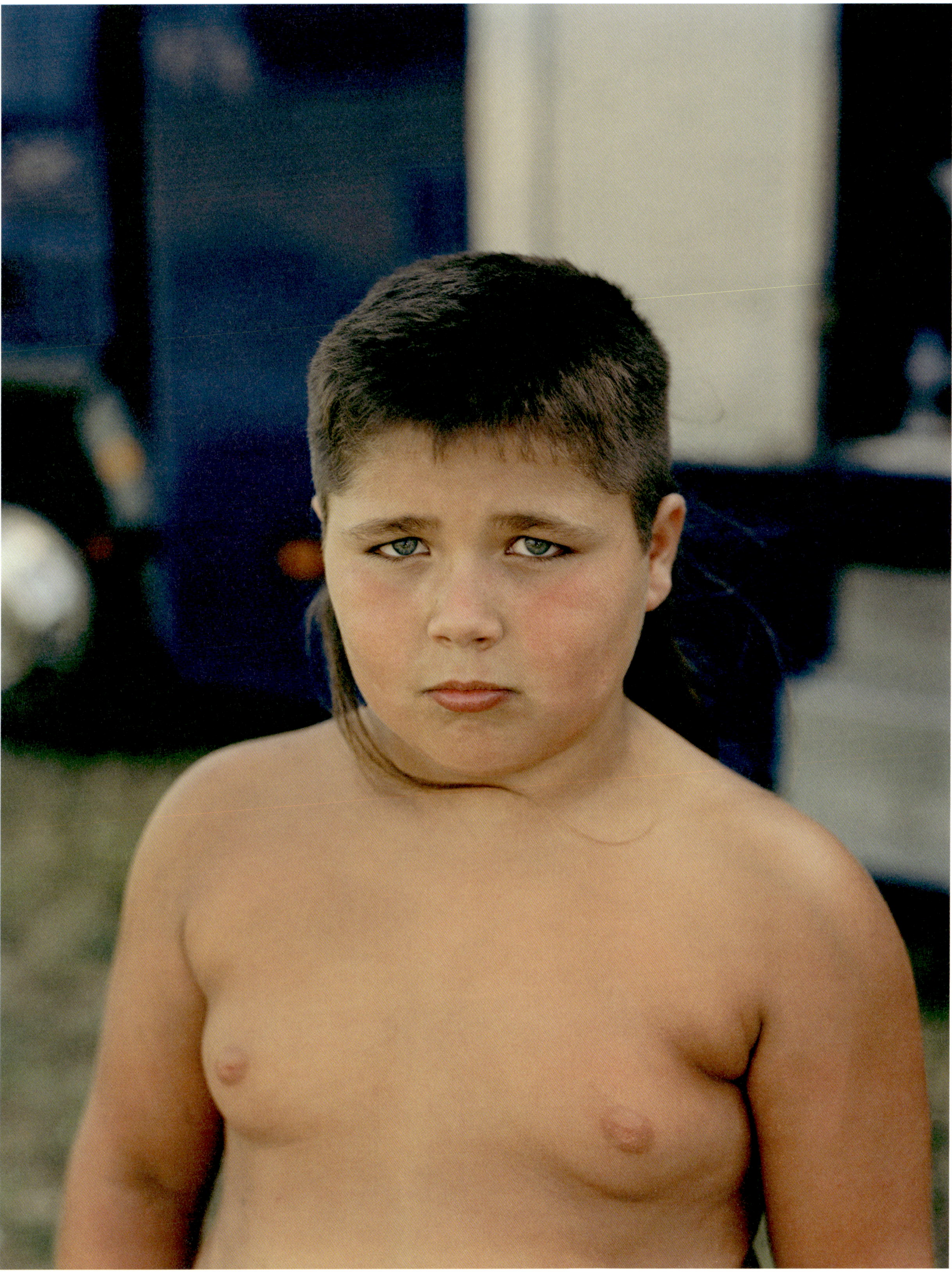

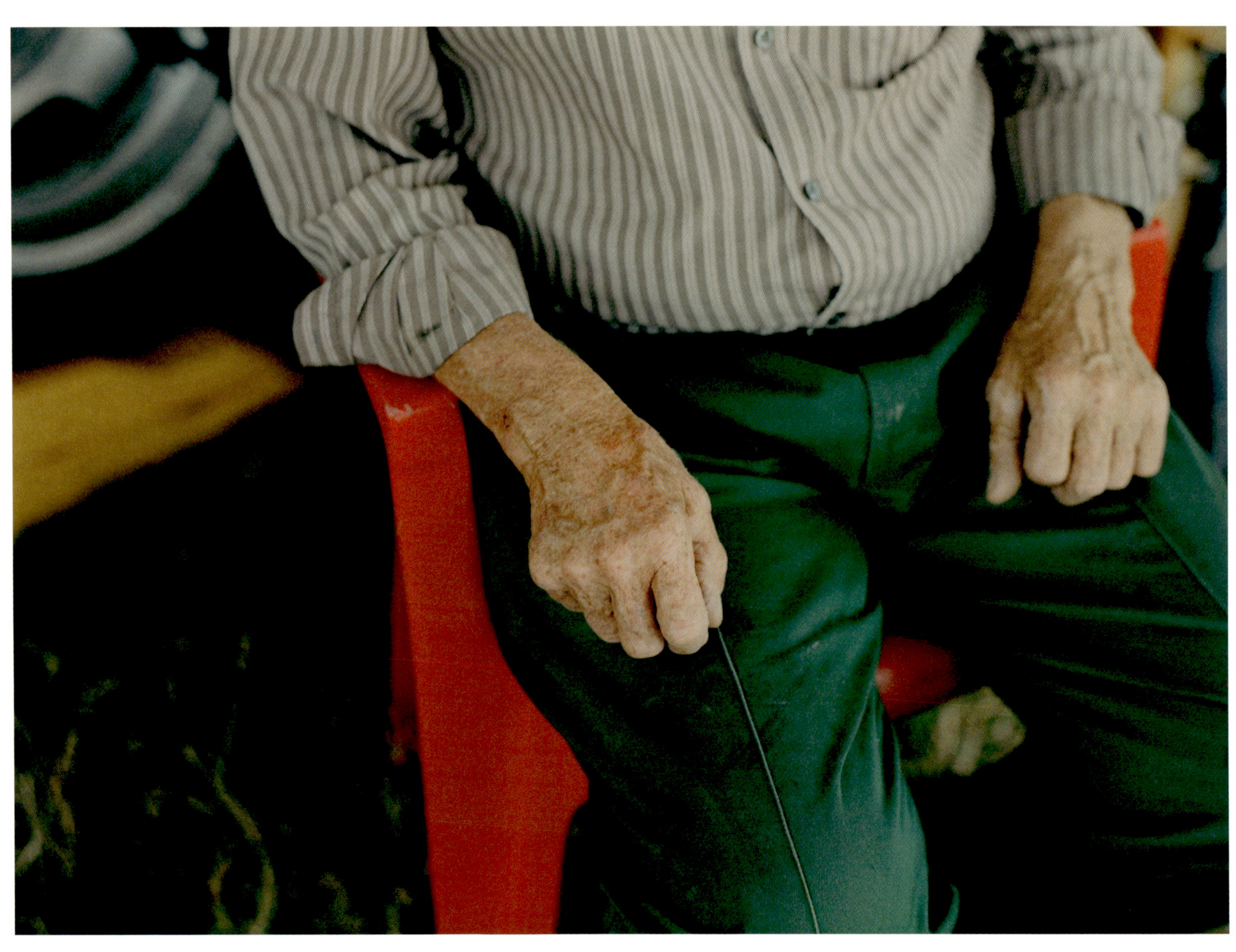

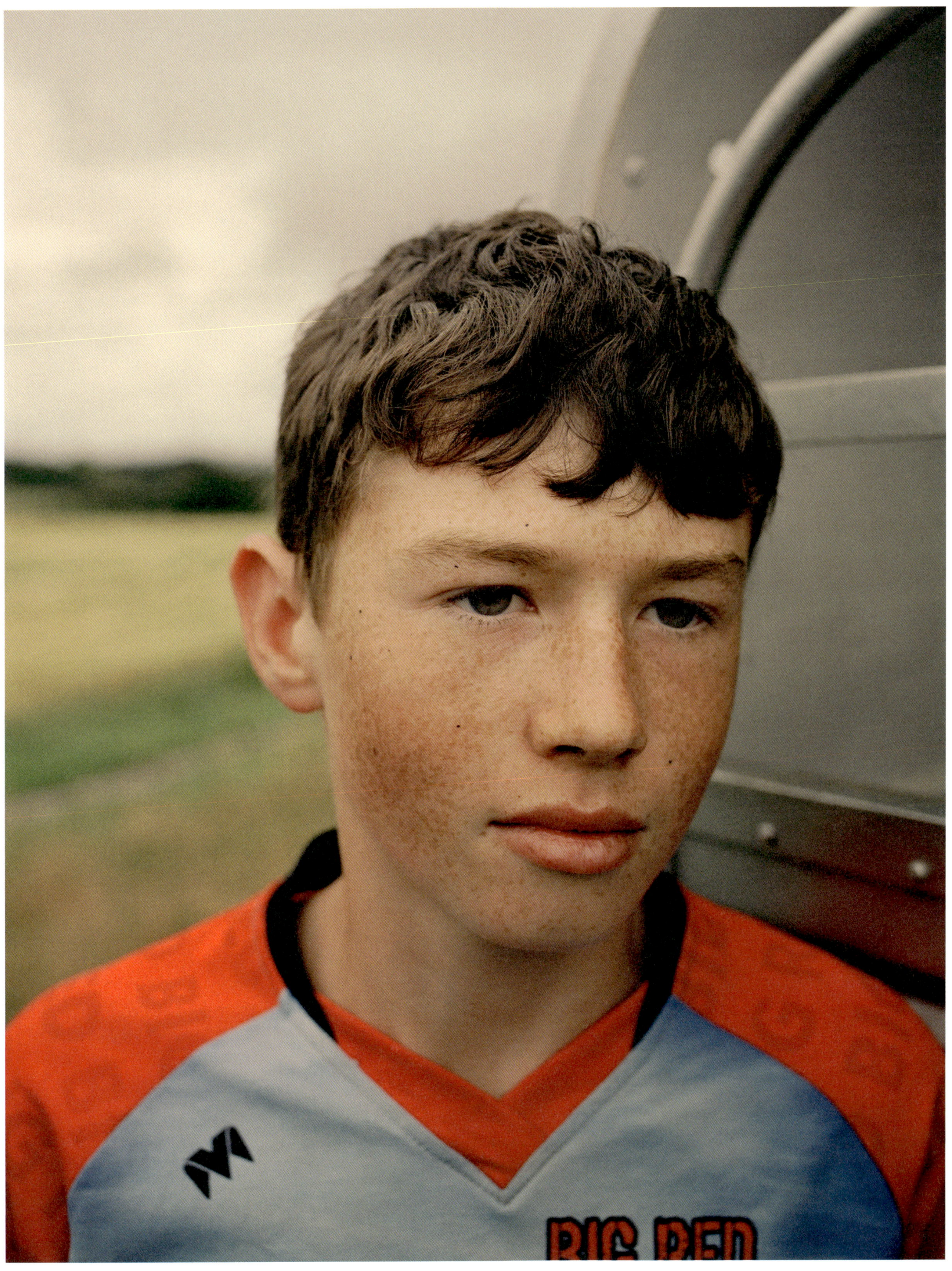
BIG RED

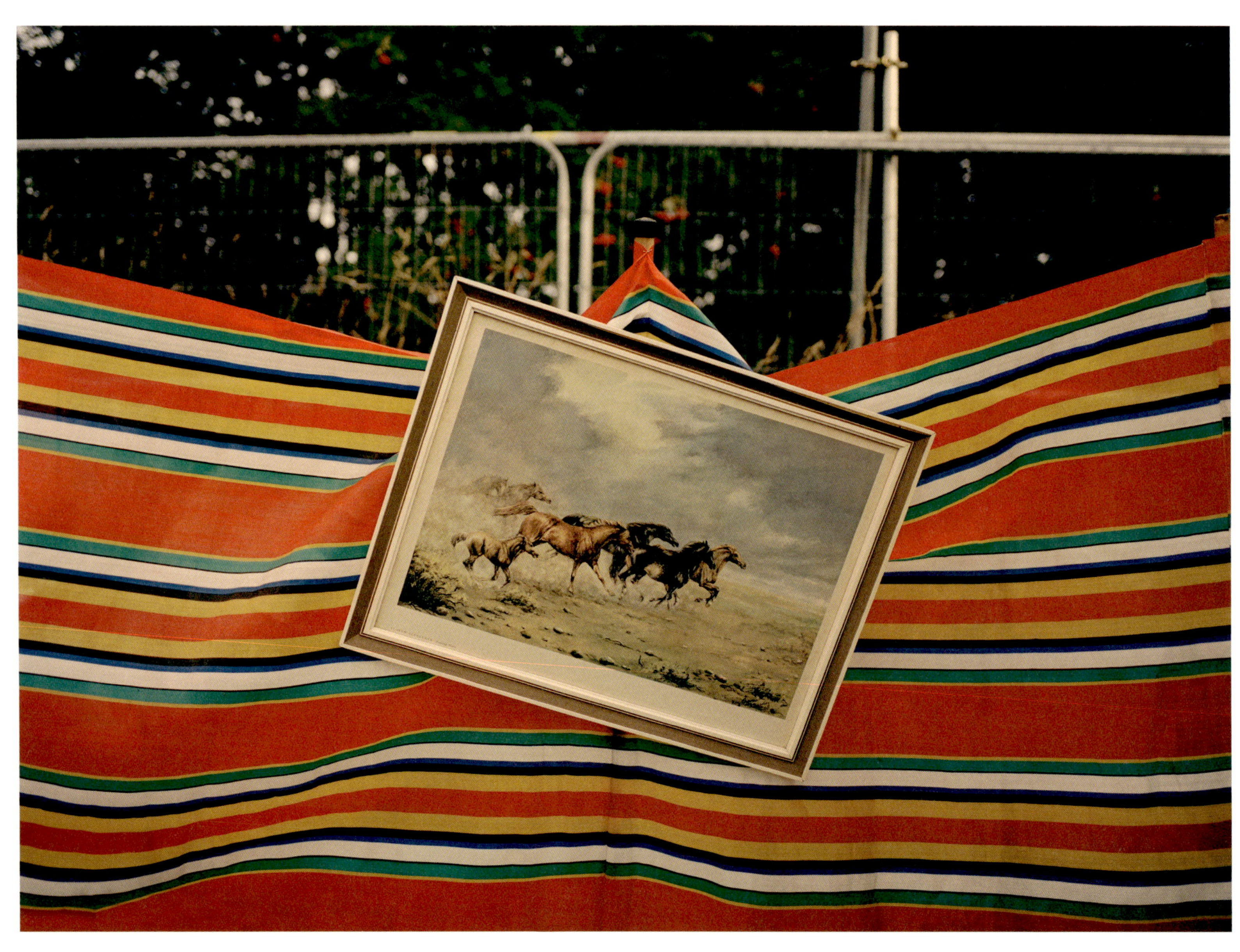

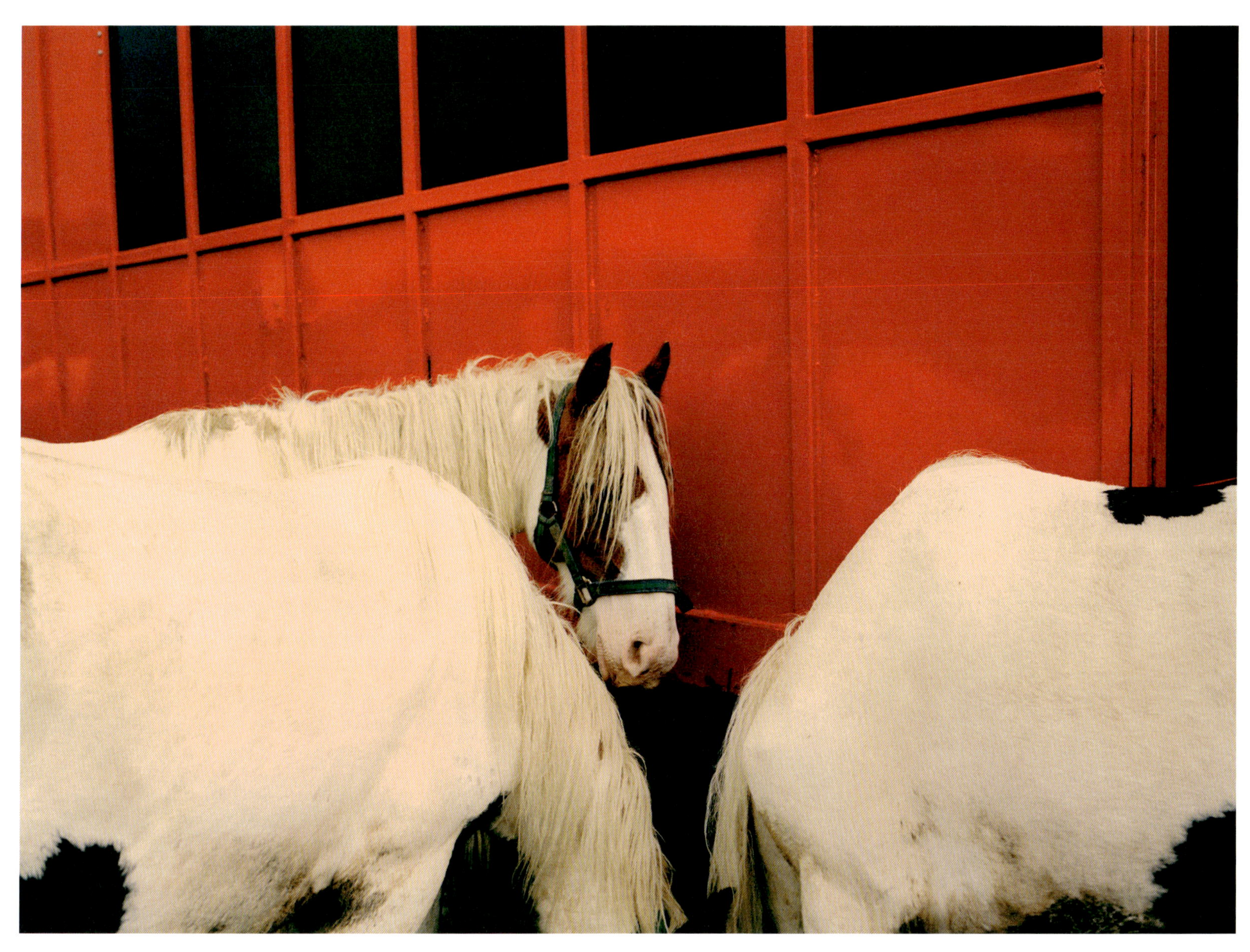

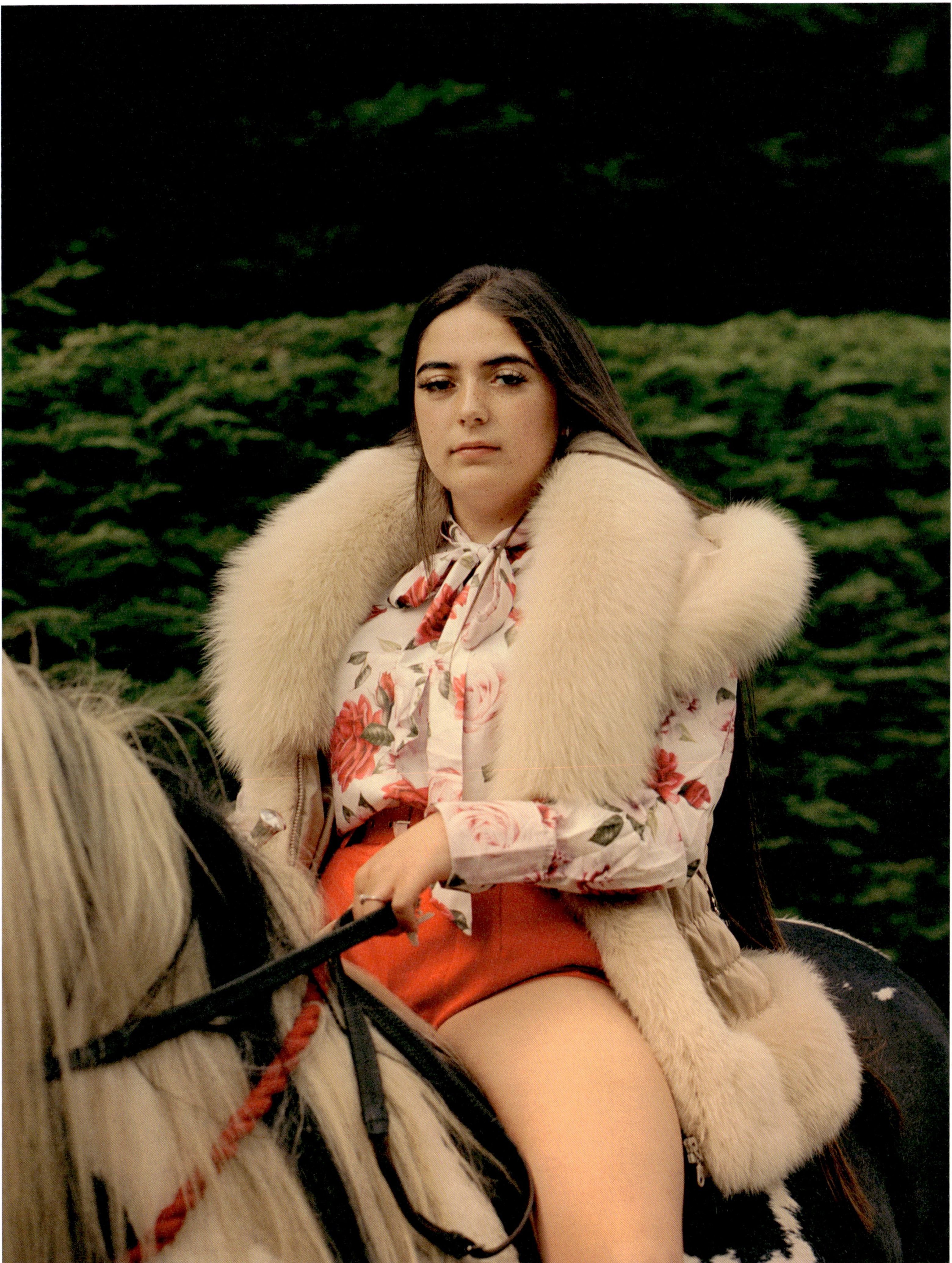

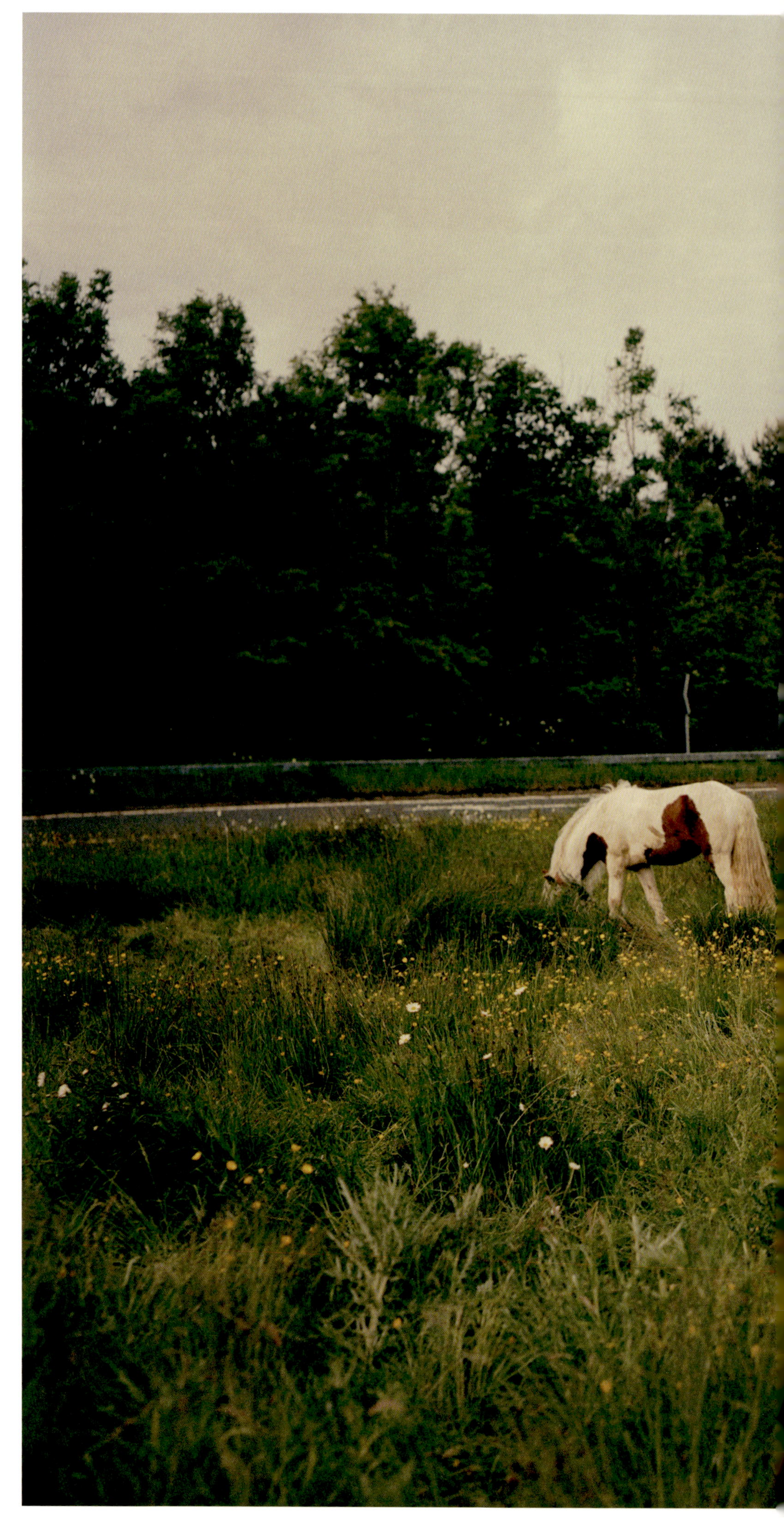

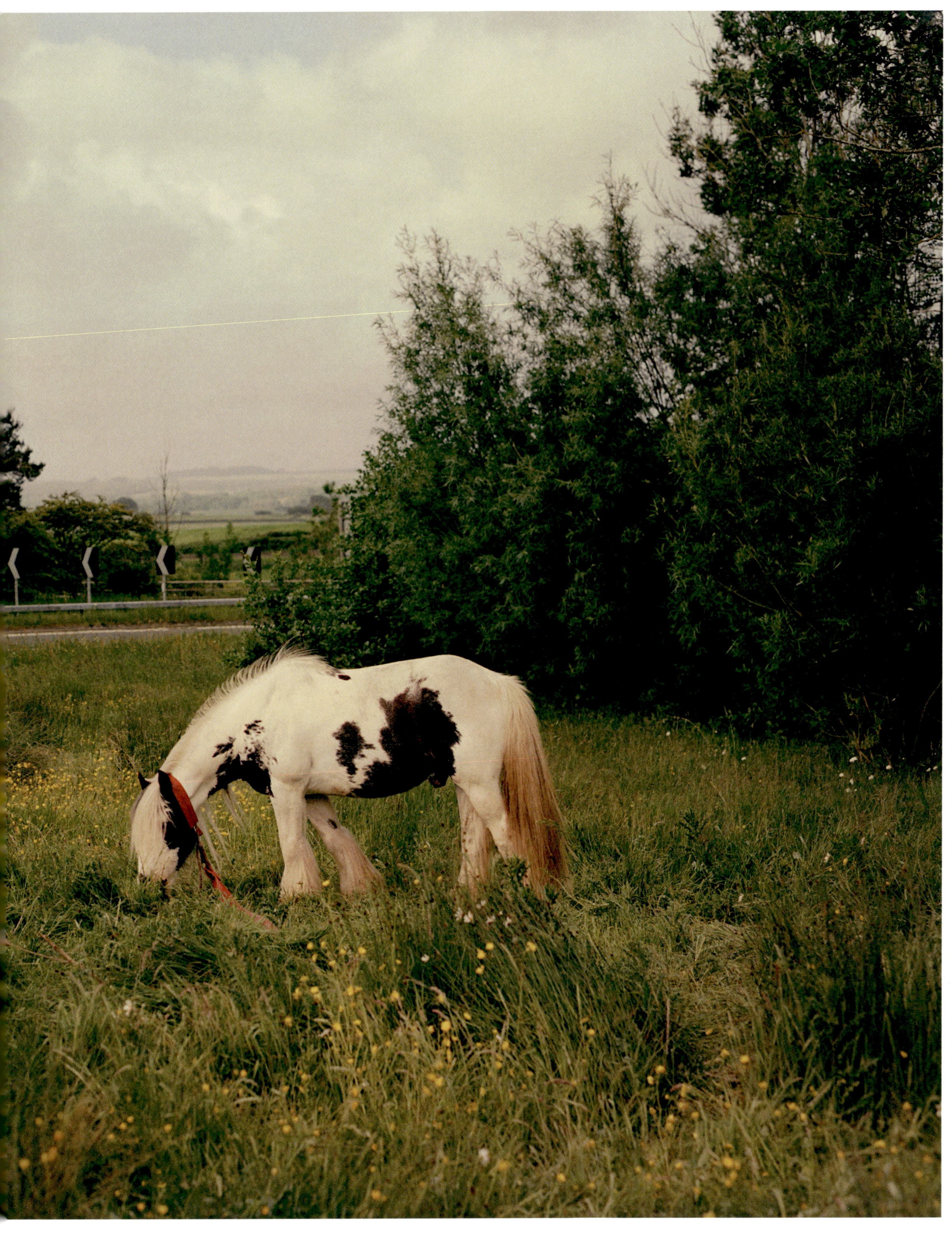

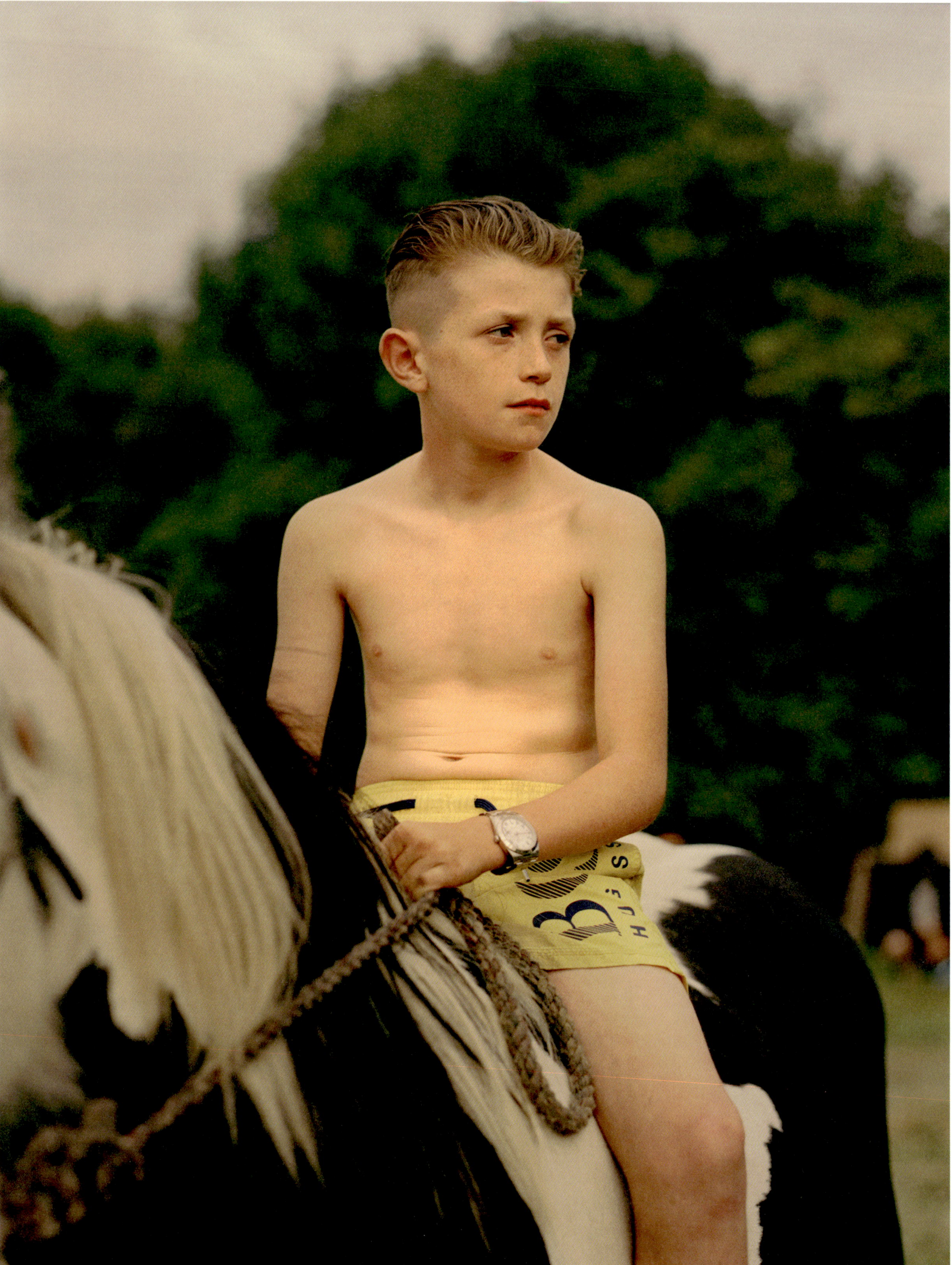

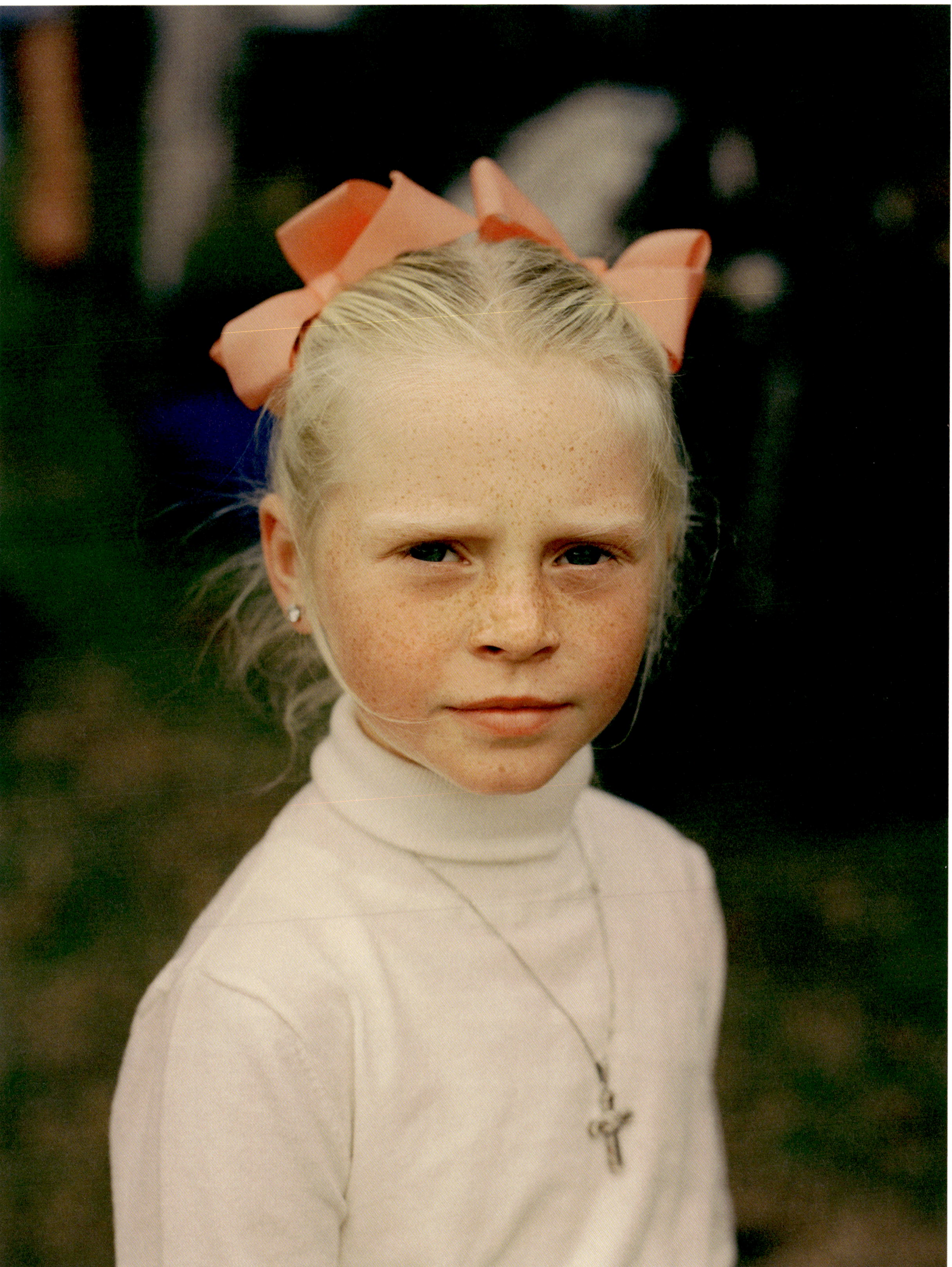

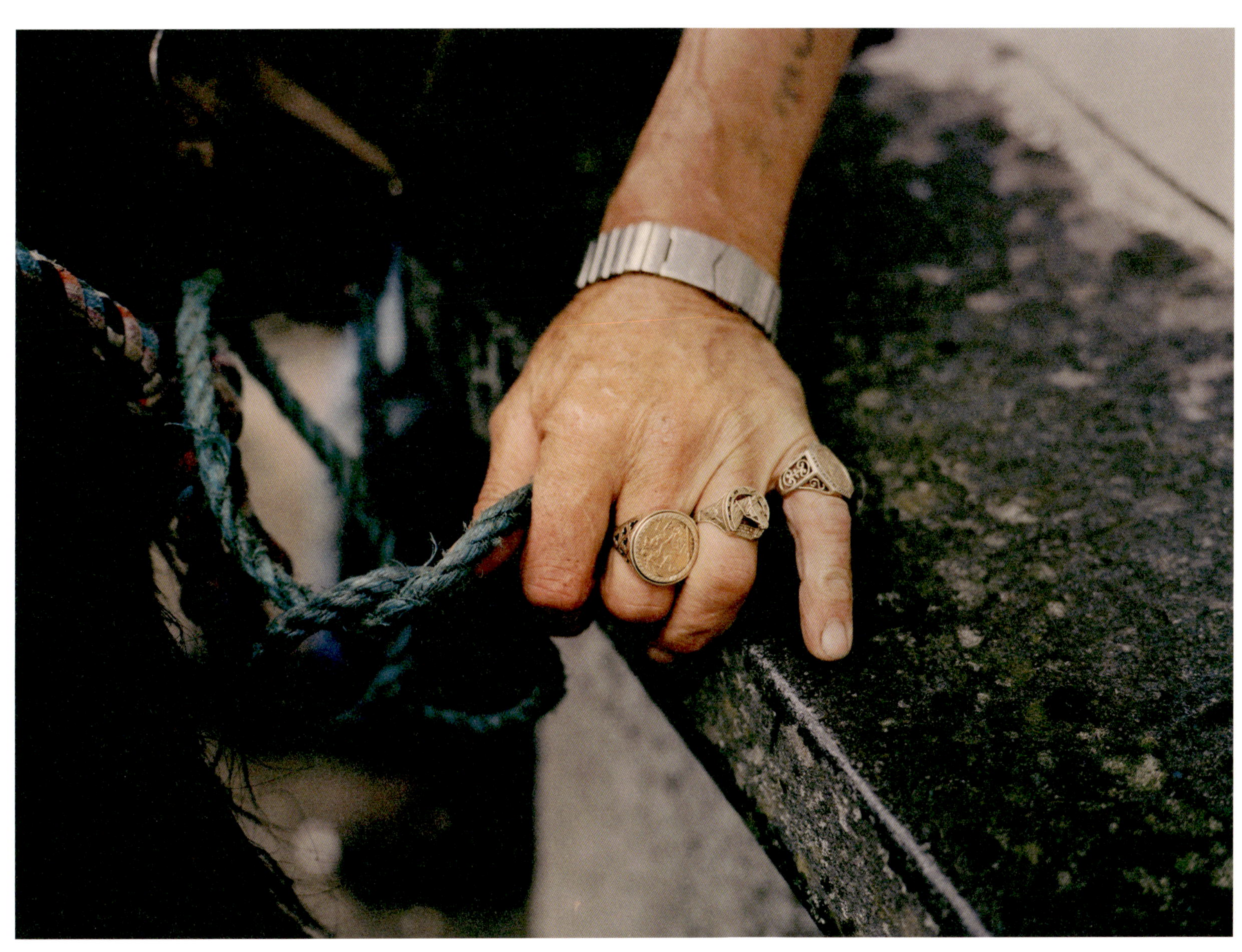

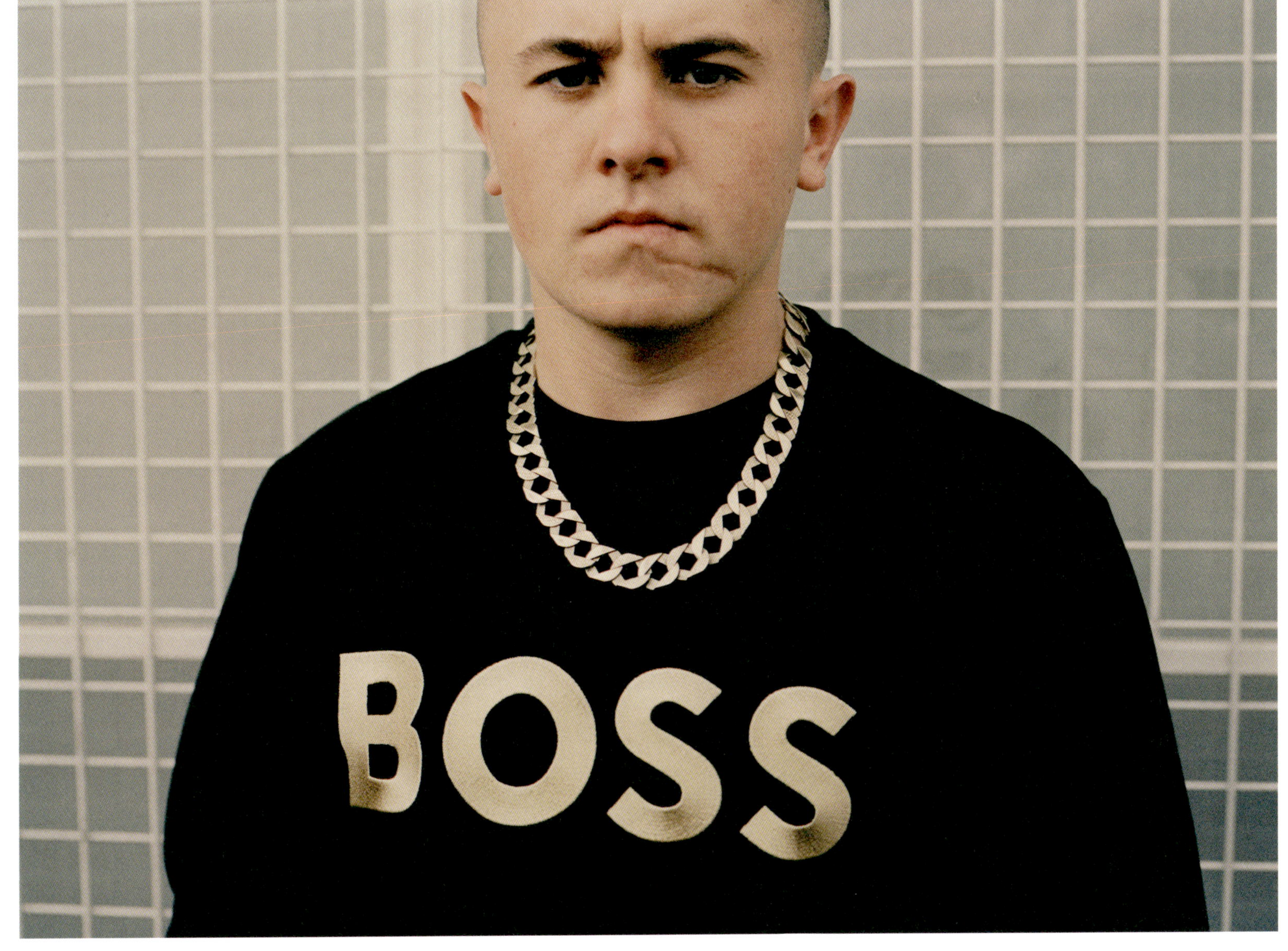
BOSS

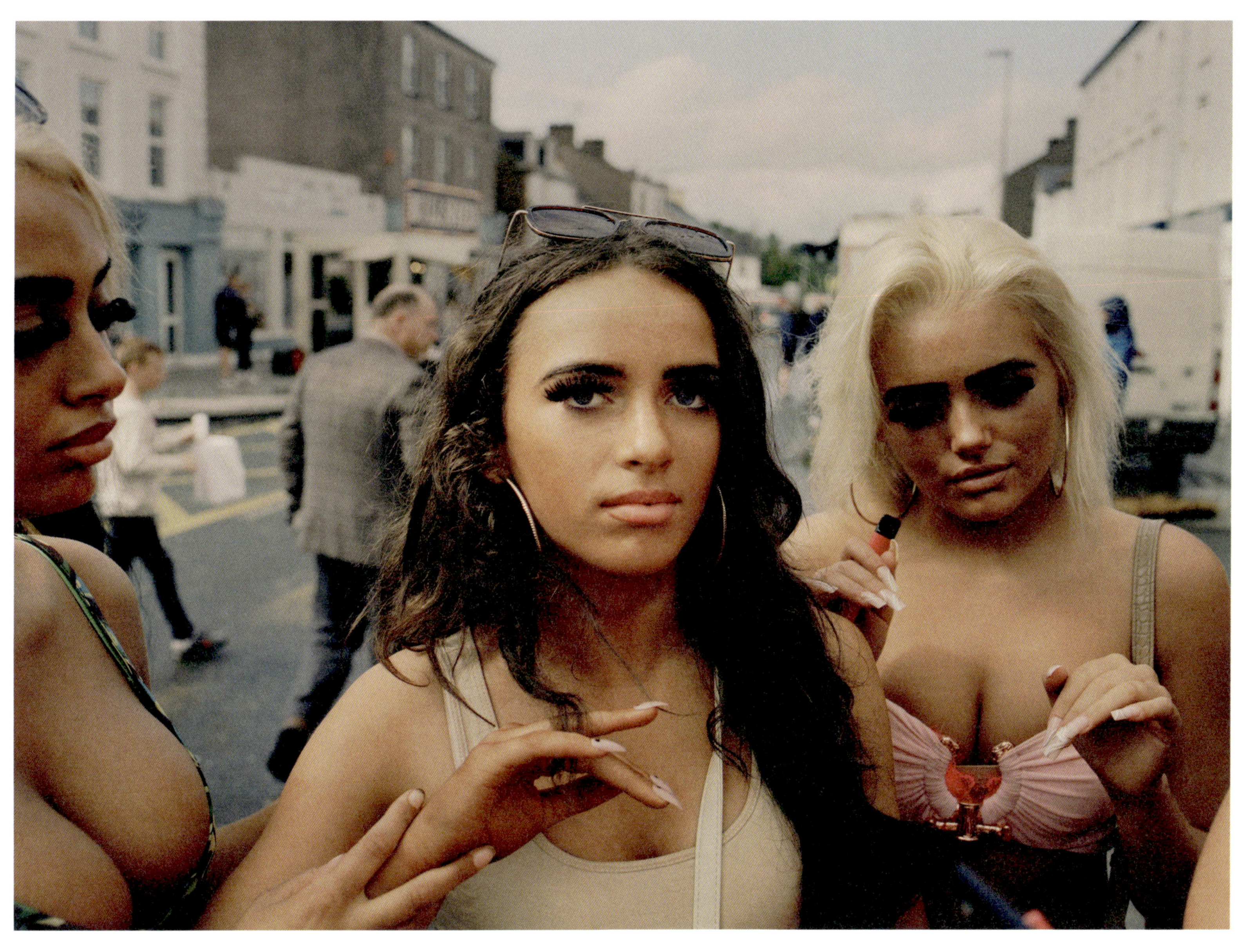

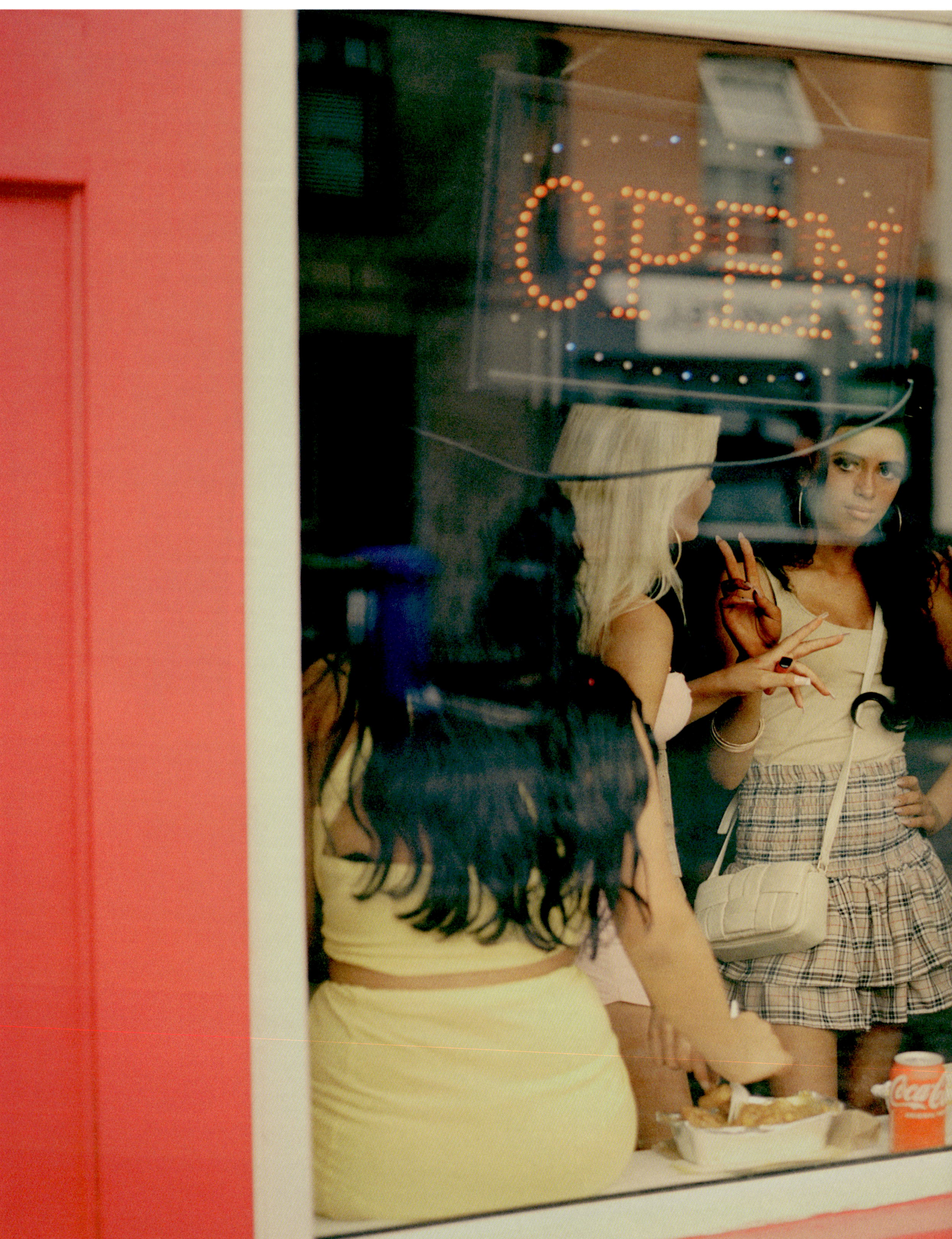
OPEN

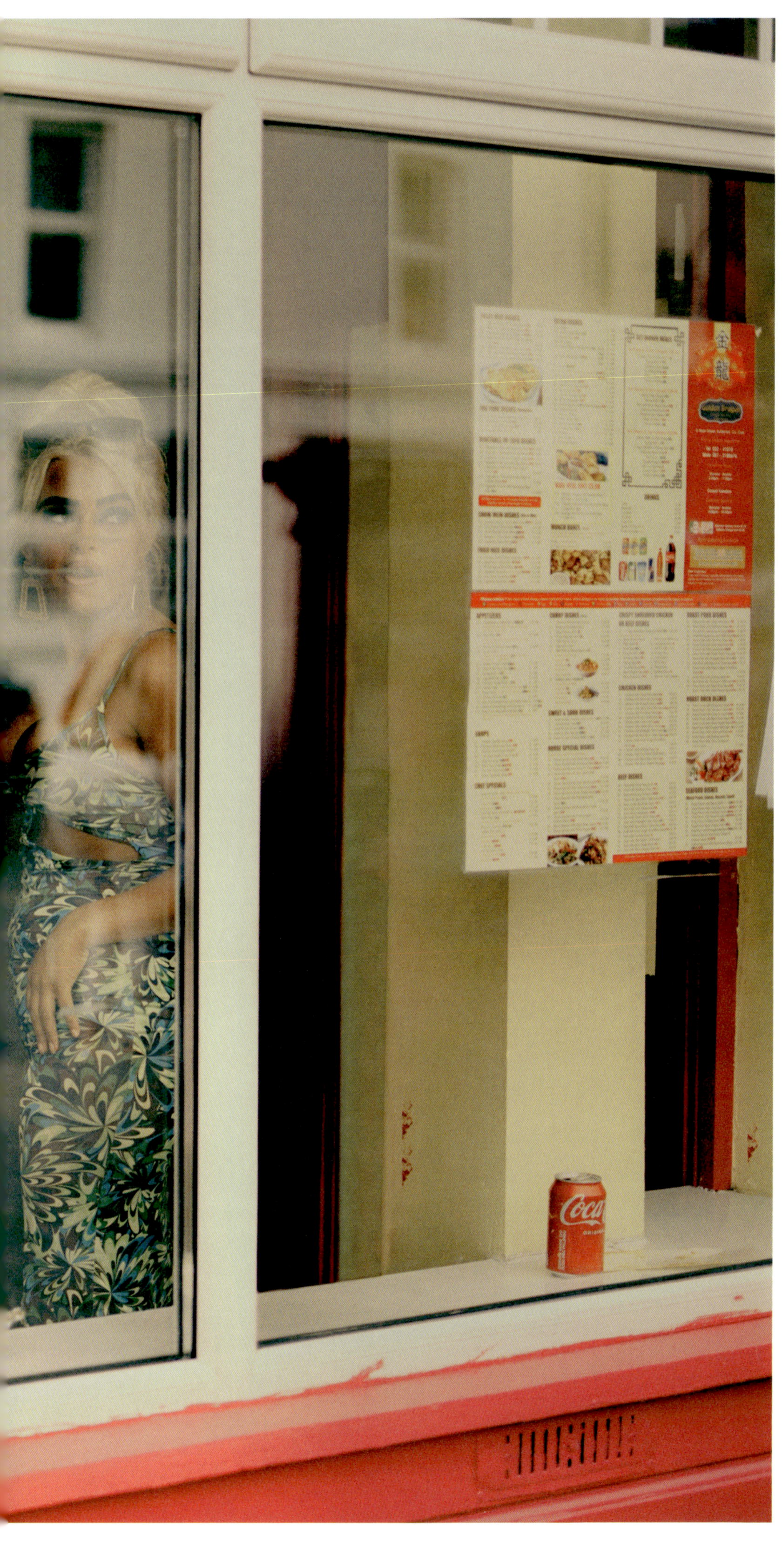
Coca

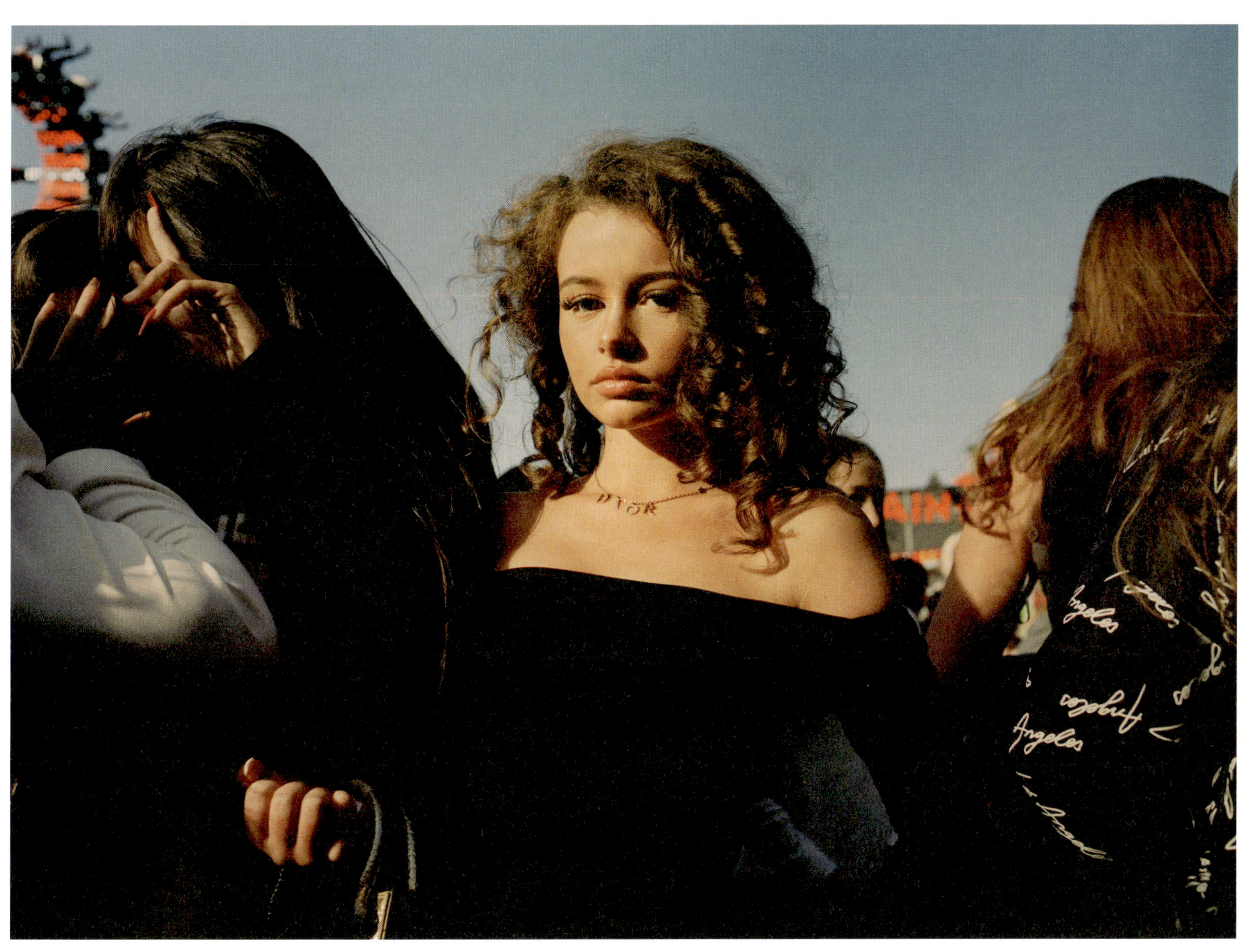
Angeles

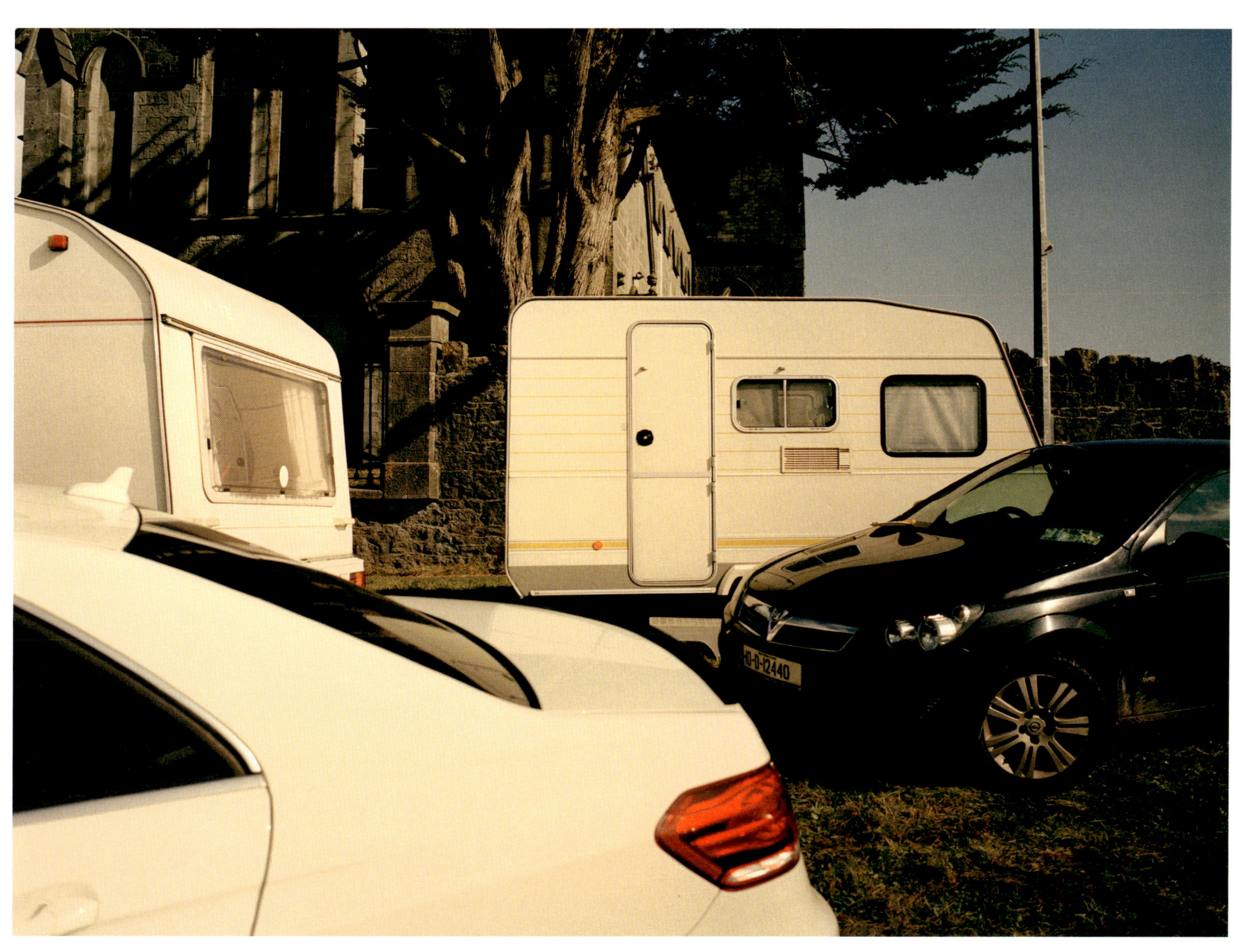
D-12440

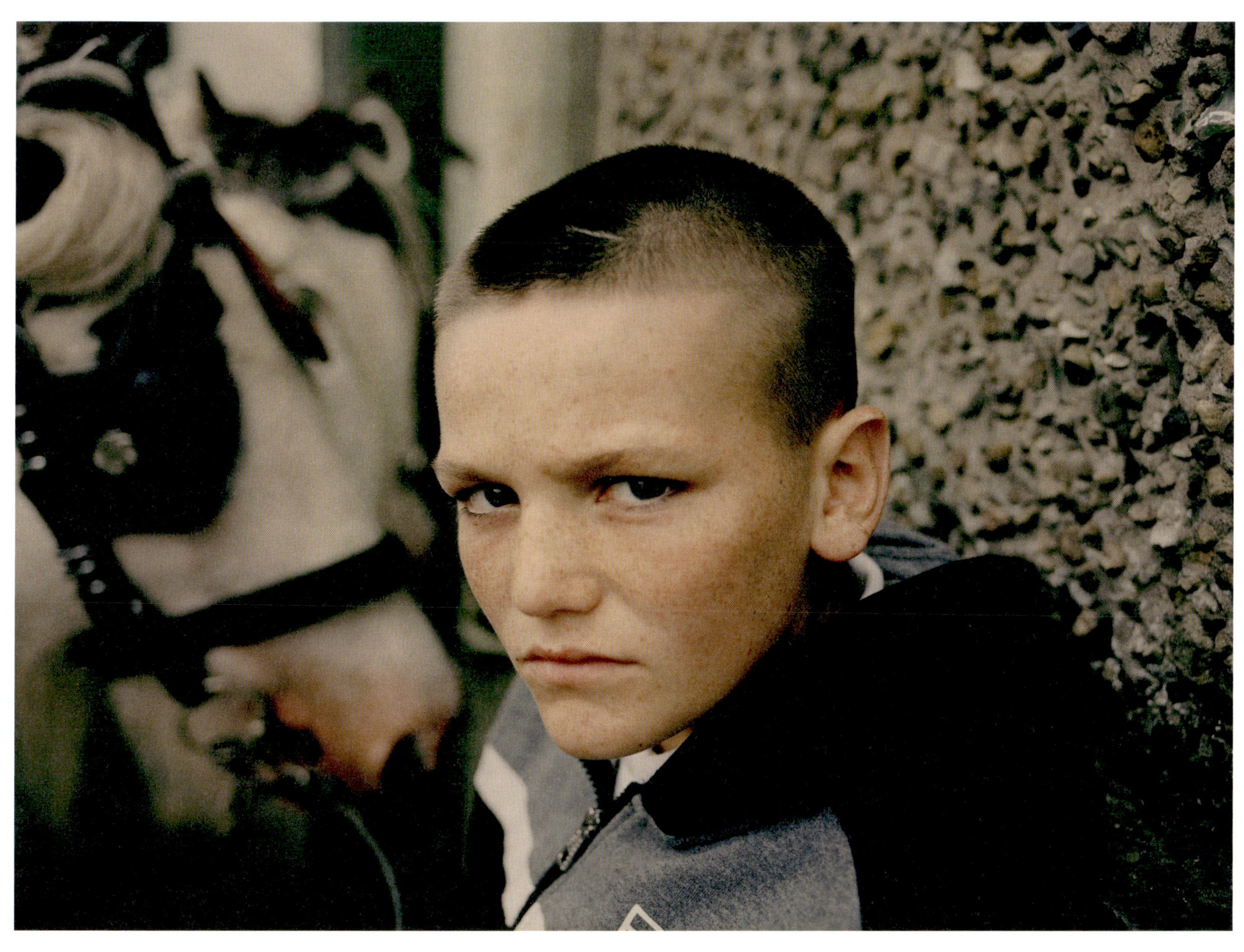

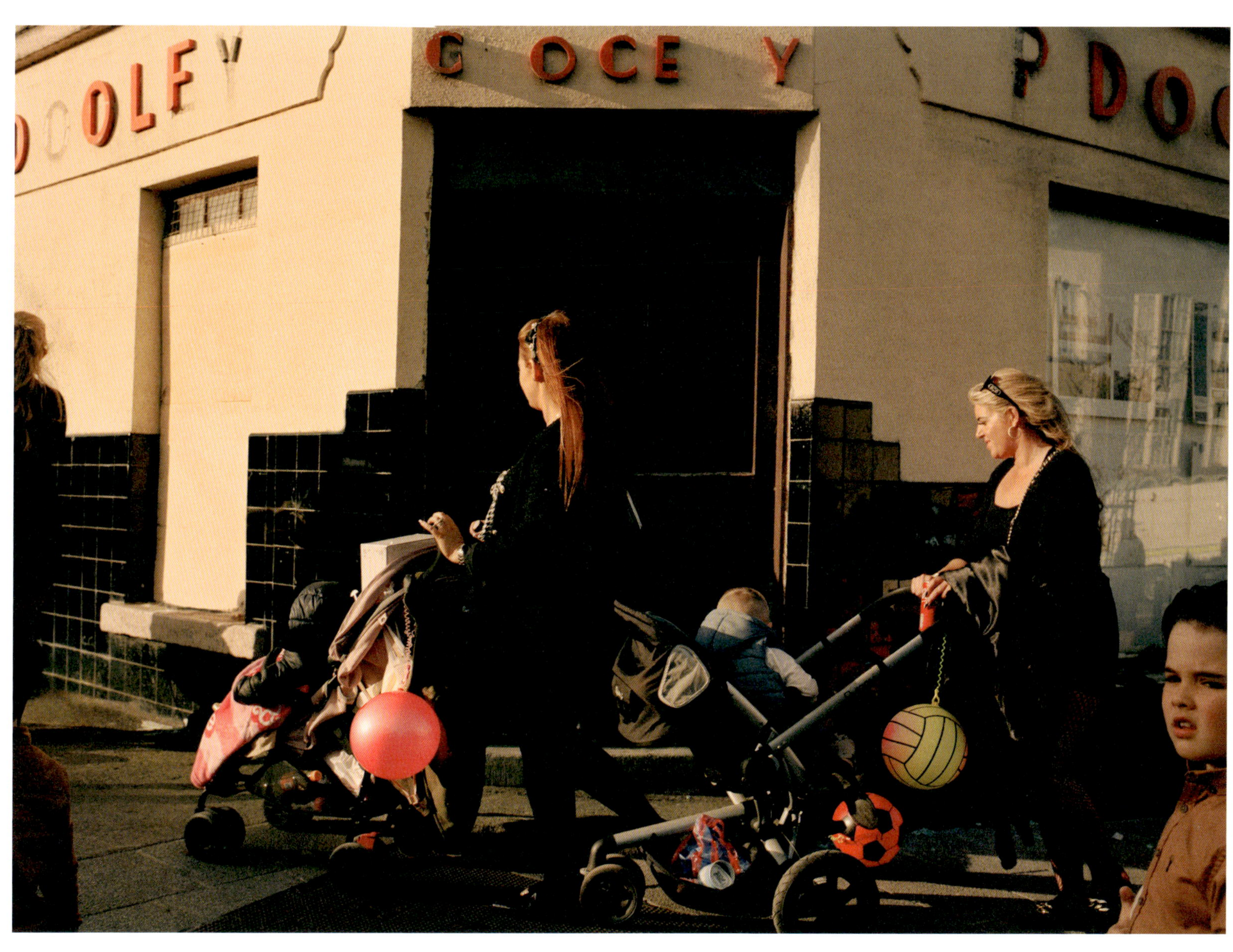

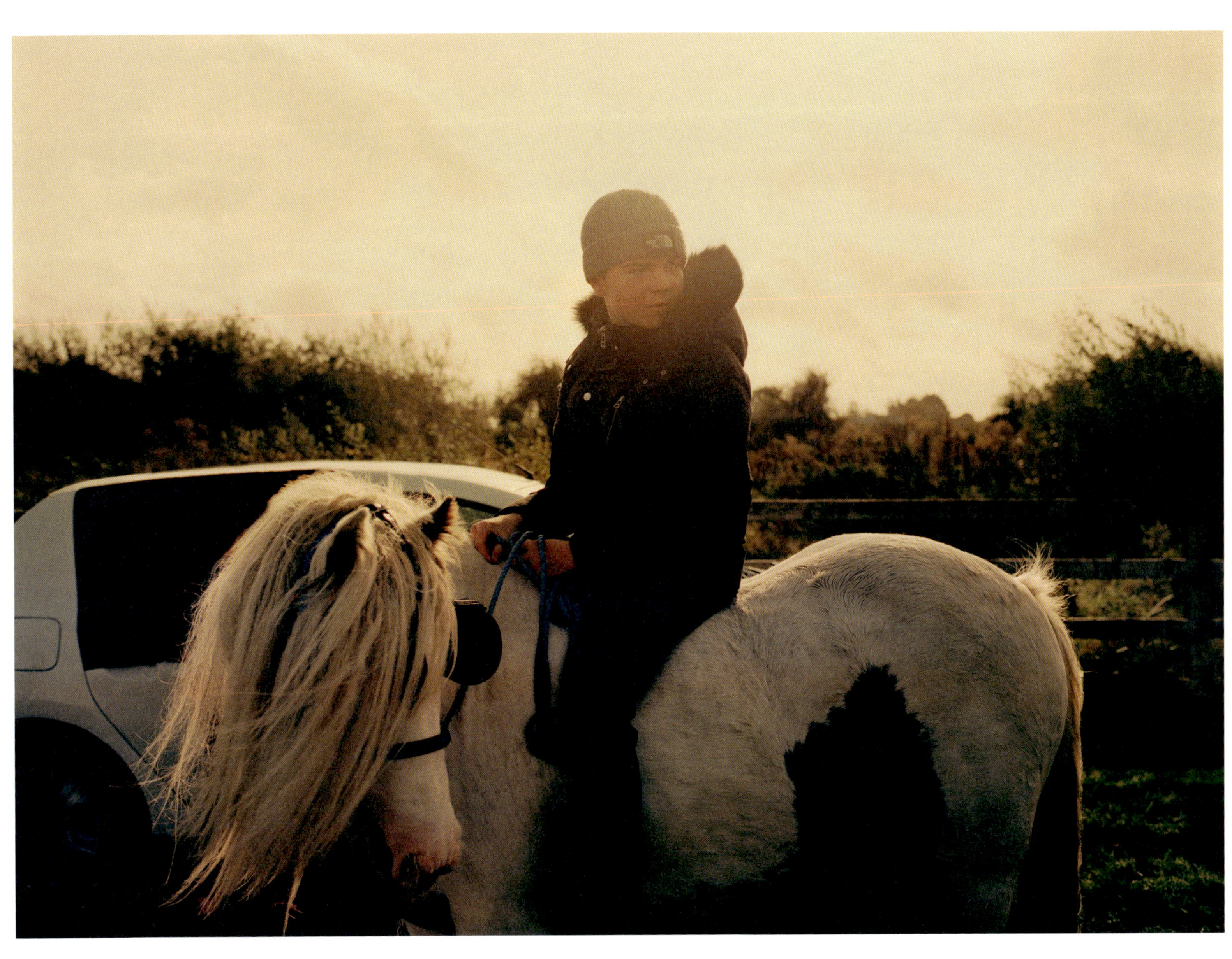

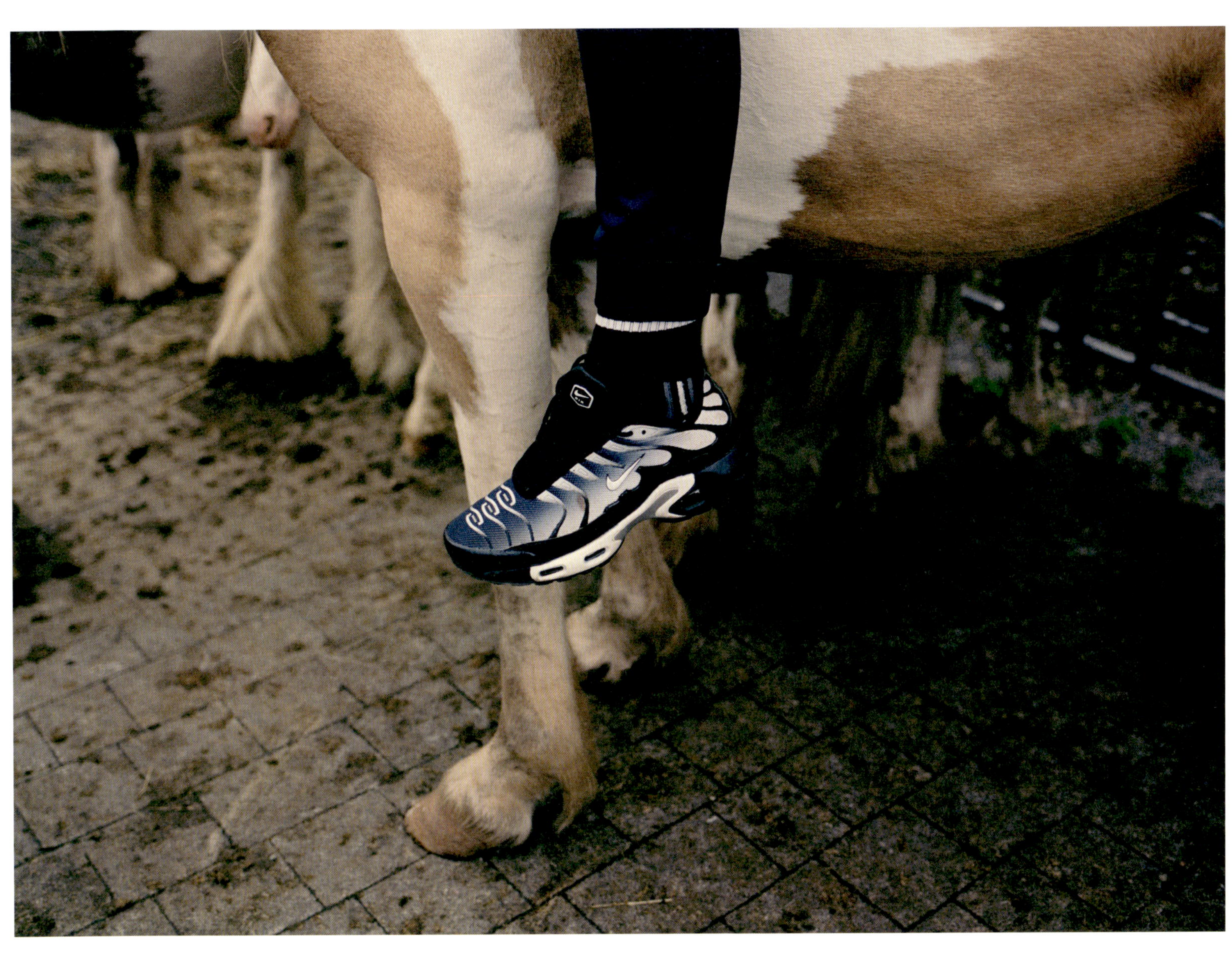

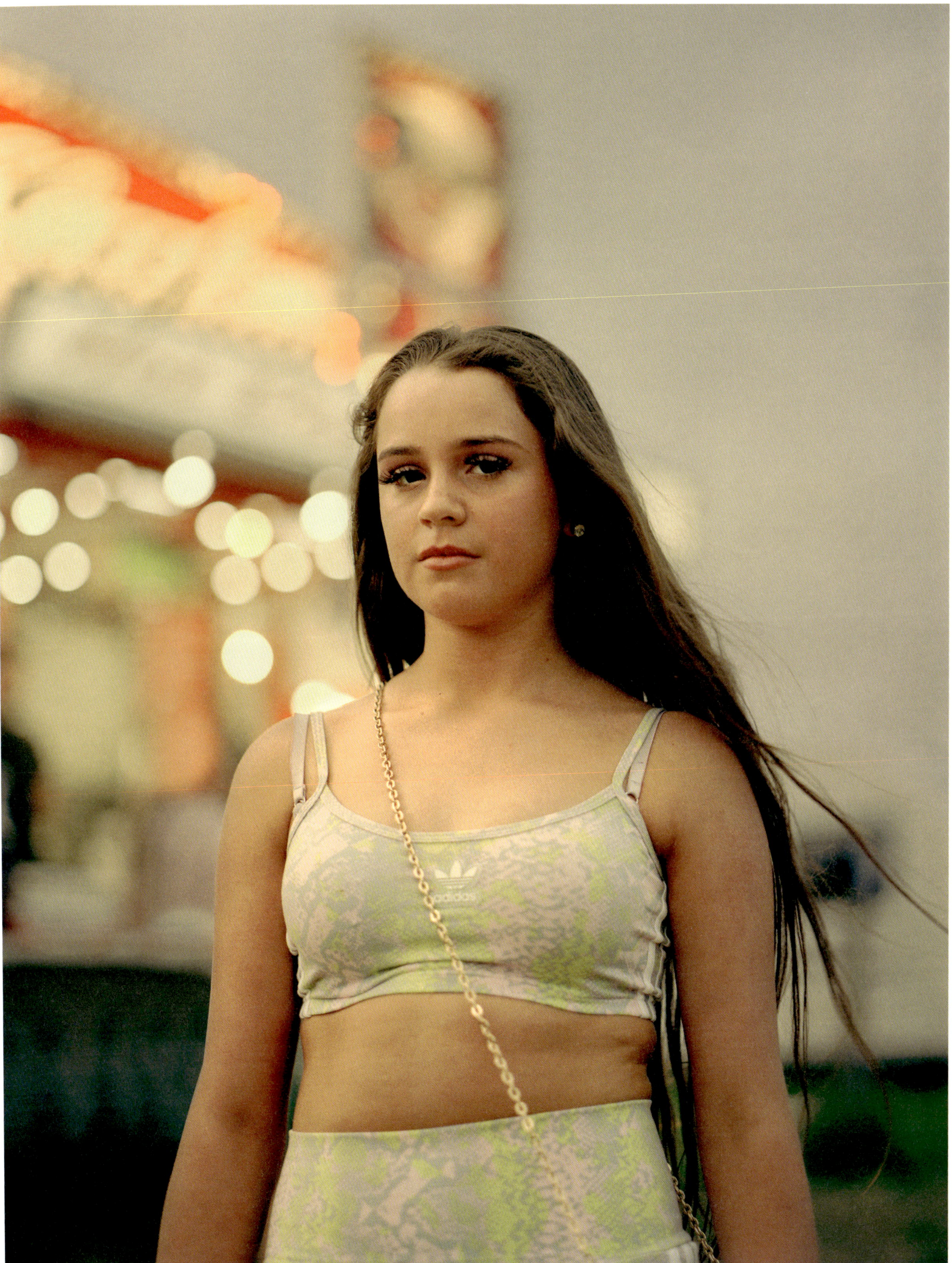
adidas

*Pillar to Post*

**Damian LeBas**

Travellers don't expect miracles in how we are depicted. We know our faults better than anyone. We don't need to be told that some people let us down, or that we let ourselves down. We're living these things, those of us who are trying our best to make a good life for ourselves and our children and to be a useful part of the world. We don't want special treatment. But we do expect people who talk about us to try and tell the truth. We expect pictures of us to tell the truth as well. And when it comes to these things, we're used to being disappointed. We've had hundreds of years of practice.

We know the camera can lie, and that it does, because the camera lies about Travellers all the time. Photographs of scenes that do not represent us, or of ephemera stripped of their context, are as dishonest as anything that the tongue or the pen can say. The one bag of rubbish left strewn across a field by a careless family, where yesterday fifty trailers and motors stood, forty-nine of which have left nothing but tracks on grass. The two lads caught fighting in the street when their two dozen less impulsive friends have already gone home for the night. The mugshot in the newspaper under a headline of 'Traveller Crime,' of someone whose brothers and sisters have never once been in trouble with the law. The camera not only lies, it might be the finest liar of them all, because we trust it like no other.

But in the right pair of hands, there's no more powerful gleaner of truth than a camera. And Sam Wright's photographs tell the truth about us. How can I make such a bold claim and know it's correct? Because Wright's photography doesn't tell one story, a flat story bereft of dimensions. His photography tells the layers. Unlike the close-minded alarmist reportage of the local newspaper reporter, sent out to gather evidence of the menace of Gypsy life, secure in their conclusions before they even get to the scene, Wright's photos are open. Every photo has edges, but the photographer gets to choose whether these edges are steel walls or blades, cutting off peripheral things that contribute their truths to the centre, or whether they are considered outer limits, merely defining the point outside which lay things that are part of a different story.

Looking at these photos, we can see the desire to let things into the frame, to keep enough within the borders that we never see the subject in isolation, brutally cut off, or deliberately apprehended in a moment of uncharacteristic darkness, a nadir of the spirit. When Wright gives us a wide image, it feels wide enough to give us a proper swath of the Traveller world, and when he gives us a portrait, there's always more in the frame than a stark, caustic and ultimately animalising depiction of a face, which we have grown accustomed to seeing from photographers who approach us with the cold glint of old-fashioned anthropology in their eye. Wright's portraits are crisp in places, but also replete where appropriate with the soulful haze of life, its uncertainty and interconnectedness. Wright waits for his subjects to give him the gaze: he doesn't just jump in and take it. Nothing is oversimplified. The gold buckle ring in sharp focus gives way to the cuddle being offered by the hand that wears it. The child counting a seemingly unlikely wad of cash is doing so in the company of the family, supervised, part of something whole. We see the softness behind the hardness, the labour behind the glamour, the struggle behind the flash. These images do not seek to showcase nomads-as-weirdoes, Travellers-as-specimens-of-social-oddness, or, with a Victorian scholar's alarmism that must now be consigned to the intellectual tip, 'the last of the authentic Romanies in a world swamped by counterfeit Gypsies.' They commemorate proud people. They hymn resilience. They offer us the human frailty that flows alongside and through the façade. He gives us no less than society: a siblinghood of citizens, whose ancestors were often seen as having little value besides being social scapegoats, or candidates for the hardest work that no one else wanted to do. And yes, many of these pictures were taken at horse fairs, and there are wagons and trailers and saddles and freshly cut hair and horseboxes and gold. You could call these things stereotypical symbols, or you could call them typical features of much modern Gypsy and Traveller life. Many of us live in houses these days, and many neither keep horses nor go to the fairs, but that doesn't affect the centrality of these things to our culture, as they have been central in the past. To feel your heart leap when you see a glimmering open lot vardo on Fair Hill at Appleby, you don't need to have lived in one, especially when your great-grandparents did. Every Traveller knows the feeling they get when they see photos of Appleby in the paper: that in a sense, we are all at the Fair, even when we're not there.

And what do we mean by society? Do we just mean 'Traveller society?' Of course we don't, because there's no such thing as an isolated society of Gypsies and Travellers. No people is an island. We're out there in the thick of life, in the fields and roads of the world, each of us living their life as they see fit. Which brings us to the most important thing that pulses within these special images—life. The life of people, my people in the ethnic sense, but also, in a sense which may be far more important, your people as well, whoever you are—because at bottom, the trials and glories of Gypsies and Travellers are no more and no less than the trials and glories of humanity, occasionally fixed in cultural focus by their appearance at the roadside, their being silhouetted by fire, their placement in the midday stocks of the tabloids or of legislation, or their caricaturing in film. Sam Wright does not supply caricatures. He gives us our bit of the world, and he does it with honour.

Huge thanks to the Traveller and Gypsy community for their welcoming warmth and openness and everyone I met that took time to chat with me, have their photo taken or welcomed me in for a cup of tea.

Special thanks to the Smith, McDonagh, Nicolson, Varey, Reilly, Moorehouse, Hunter, Doherty, Haywood, Whitehead, Connor, Evans, Shailes, Heyes, Booth, Barras, Cooper, Chapman, Wallace, Curtin, James, Chapman, Pease, Jordan and McCarthy families.

Big thanks to my family, Si Lakos, Billy Wright, LGA Team, Dennis Tuffnell, Louis Almond, Vlad Barin and Ben Goulder.

*Pillar to Post*
First published in 2024
by GOST Books, London

info@gostbooks.com
gostbooks.com



Edited and designed by GOST:
Rossella Castello, Katie Clifford, Gemma Gerhard, Justine Hucker, Allon Kaye, Eleanor Macnair, Claudia Paladini, Ana Rocha

Printed in Italy by EBS

British Library cataloguing-in-publication data.
A catalogue record of this book is available from the British Library.

ISBN 978-1-915423-53-5

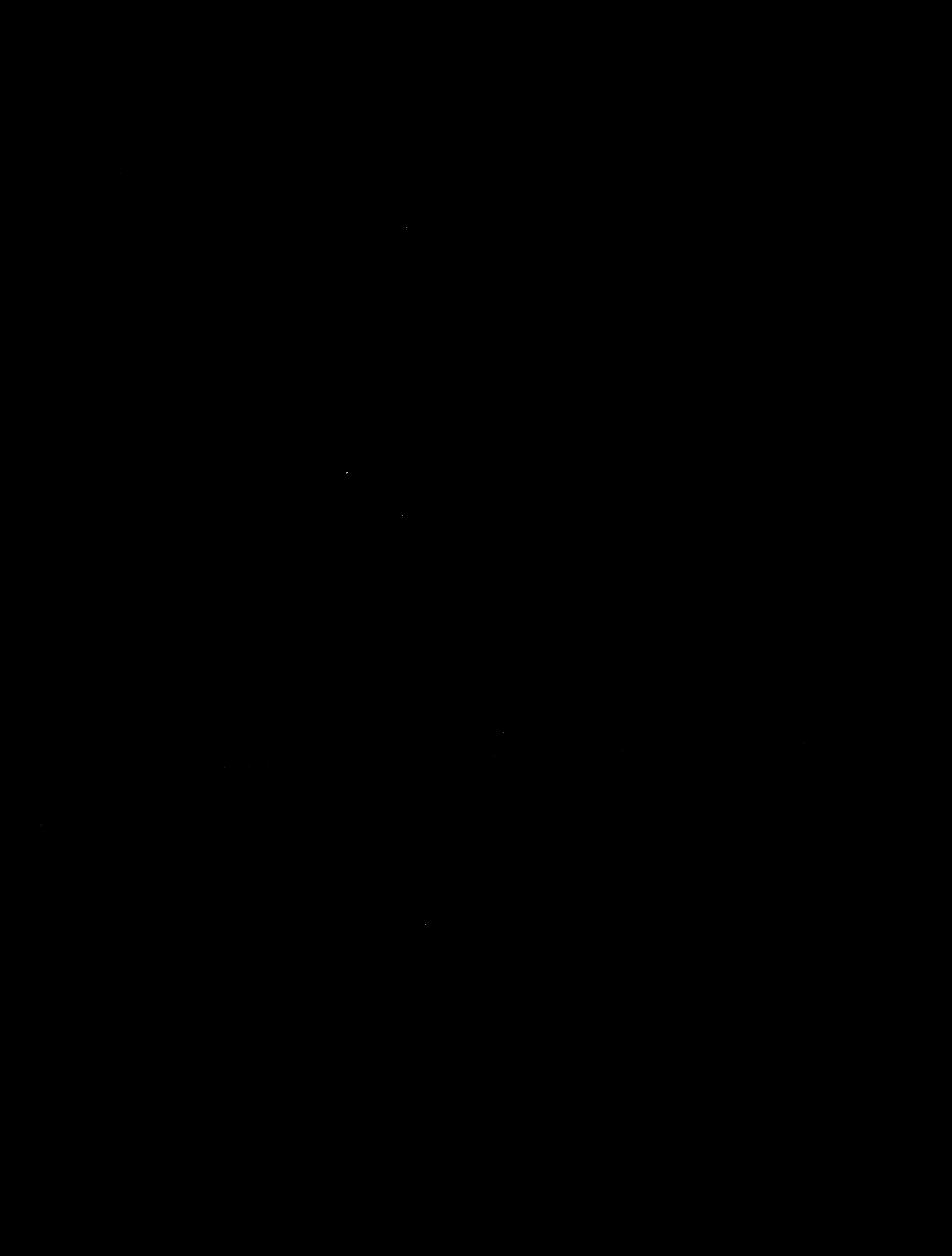

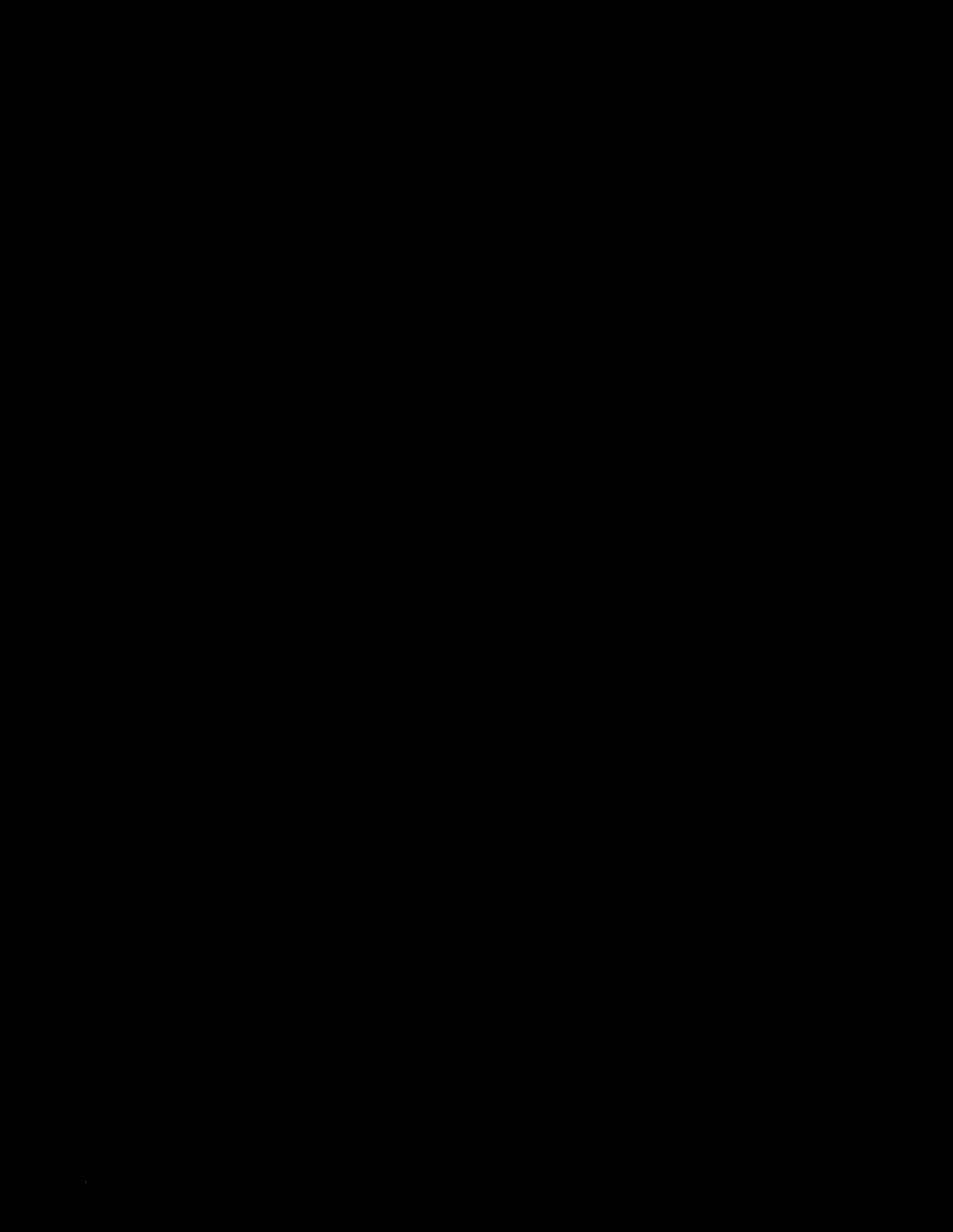